A POWER SHIFT IN PUBLIC EDUCATION
Seven Strategies for Dealing with Broken Promises

Herbert F. Pandiscio

ROWMAN & LITTLEFIELD EDUCATION
Lanham • New York • Toronto • Plymouth, UK

Published in the United States of America
by Rowman & Littlefield Education
A Division of Rowman & Littlefield Publishers, Inc.
A wholly owned subsidiary of The Rowman & Littlefield Publishing Group, Inc.
4501 Forbes Boulevard, Suite 200, Lanham, Maryland 20706
www.rowmaneducation.com

Estover Road
Plymouth PL6 7PY
United Kingdom

British Library Cataloguing in Publication Information Available

Library of Congress Cataloging-in-Publication Data

Pandiscio, Herbert F. (Herbert Frederick), 1931–
  A power shift in public education : seven strategies for dealing with broken promises /
Herbert F. Pandiscio.
    p. cm.
  Includes bibliographical references.
  ISBN 978-1-60709-241-4 (cloth : alk. paper)
  ISBN 978-1-60709-242-1 (pbk. : alk. paper)
  ISBN 978-1-60709-243-8 (electronic)
  1. Public schools—United States. 2. Educational change—United States. I. Title.
  LA217.2.P36 2009
  371.010973—dc22   2009004552

∞™ The paper used in this publication meets the minimum requirements of American
National Standard for Information Sciences—Permanence of Paper for Printed Library
Materials, ANSI/NISO Z39.48-1992.

Manufactured in the United States of America.

"Written in clear and concise language, this is a great resource for all who are interested in making great schools, not just better schools. *A Power Shift in Public Education* bypasses educational jargon, making it a wonderful read and resource for boards of education as well as parents and the general public. It answers the question, 'What makes an excellent school district, and how do we create it?' This is a book about big ideas. It is both foundational and visionary."

—**Pamela Gourlie**, former chairperson,
East Haddam Board of Education, Connecticut

"A variety of readers will find provocative Pandiscio's bold claim that a commitment to educational excellence through genuinely successful schools, which help each child equally to realize full intellectual potential, will renew the United States' global prominence in the twenty-first century. He radically suggests that people are to blame for unsuccessful schools—not limited resources, curricula, or programs. Pandiscio's voice of experience proves convincing and reassuring as he delineates specific strategies for responsible leadership rooted in a fundamental belief that successful education must be truly intellectual and excellent."

—**Margaret O. Killinger**, Rezendes Preceptor for the Arts,
Honors College at the University of Maine, and author of
The Good Life of Helen K. Nearing

"The seven strategies described in this book are all about leadership. It is heartening that these strategies do not have to cost anything to implement. No new programs need to be developed and no new equipment or educational materials are required. While you may not agree with the all that is suggested by the author, it is hard to disagree with the notion that the teaching of reading, math, and science is the highest priority for our school systems. The challenge is for the individual running the system to have the courage to take the leadership risks necessary to make academic success happen."

—**Joanne Beers**, President of the Avon
Educational Foundation

"I enjoyed every page of *A Power Shift in Public Education*. It made me want to come out of retirement and help make a difference. Pandiscio's writing is clear, organized, and understandable. The voice of this book is bold, knowledgeable, and inspiring! The seven strategies are beautifully articulated and provide a challenge to educators at all levels. As provocative as this book is, it contains creative solutions to ensure educational excellence for all students. This is a courageous and confident writing from a leader public education has been waiting for."

—**Patricia Smith**, retired intermediate school principal

"*A Power Shift in Public Education* is written by someone with vast experience as a leader in the field. It should be used as a core reading in graduate courses in leadership. Herb Pandiscio, a retired superintendent, asks the critical questions that are so often avoided by those of us who are grappling with today's critical issues in education. He leads us to think about the 'unthinkable,' and helps place current issues in a broad historical, economic, and cultural context. While nobody, including me, will agree with everything in this book, any school leader, board of education member, policy maker, teacher, or parent will find that it stimulates them to think in new ways."

—**Mark Cohan**, superintendent of
schools/headmaster, Norwich Free Academy

"Herbert F. Pandiscio has brought powerful and thoughtful ideas to the field of public education for forty years. *A Power Shift in Public Education* is a clear demonstration of his educational expertise, his wonderful writing skills, and his ability to think big and far ahead. If some of his ideas are provocative or controversial, then so be it. As a former board member, I was not offended. This book should be required reading for every board of education member everywhere."

—**Monte J. Hopper**, former chairman,
Avon Board of Education, Connecticut

To Sarah, Alex, Meg, and Jack:
May you always attend schools and colleges where
academic achievement is the highest priority.

Contents

Foreword

I FIRST MET THE AUTHOR IN HIS ROLE as a search consultant who brought me to Connecticut twice and then as a general consultant who assisted me in revamping the human relations operation in my school system. Herb Pandiscio is not just a man on the street with an uninformed opinion about public schools. His credentials are impressive, as you will discover while reading this book. Do I agree with all that is written in this book? I do not, and you will not. But it has given me pause to reflect about my own district. Facing up to what is wrong with public education is difficult, but it must be done. It takes courage to lead, to advocate for change.

If you are a board member, superintendent, a "wanna-be" superintendent, a parent, university professor, teacher, union representative, or just someone who cares about education, you will want to read this book. It is respectful of those who lead education, those who teach in education, and the men and women who are building principals and who are on the front line every day. On the other hand, the author takes great issue with many current practices. Board of education members and school superintendents will find the book provocative but useful.

This book challenges traditions and it will challenge you. It will upset many because of the author's belief that there must be a shift of power in a school system and a dramatic change in how we compensate teachers and superintendents.

If you care about education and are open to new ideas and opinions, you must read this book.

                                                    Doris J. Kurtz, Ed.D.
                                                    Superintendent of Schools
                                                    New Britain, Connecticut

Preface

Educational Shortcomings

A S YOU READ THROUGH THESE CHAPTERS, it will be apparent that there is some degree of criticism as related to the shortcomings of board of education members, school superintendents, and teachers in addressing the problems in our schools. You may also develop the impression that the author does not have respect for them. Nothing could be further from the truth.

For twenty-five years I worked as a public school superintendent, after which I became a job search consultant in education. Prior to becoming a superintendent, I was an assistant superintendent in a large suburban district, principal of a junior-senior high school in an extremely wealthy seacoast town, and an assistant principal in a tough, large regional high school in rural upstate New York. Before that, I was a teacher, department chairperson, and assistant track coach. For six years while superintendent, I taught at two universities as an adjunct professor. Education has been my lifework, and I admire those who serve, lead, and work in it. I would never disparage them professionally, but I am willing to point out our shortcomings.

Objectives of the Book

One of the objectives of this book is to highlight the slow progress being made to make our schools successful for all students in ways that dramatically improve student learning. This book is not meant to be overly provocative or controversial. Simply said, when you examine the inability of the public school system to raise student achievement to an acceptable level across the nation, you will be deeply concerned about the future of our nation. When schools fail children, they fail the nation.

Role of Government

It has to be apparent to educators nationwide that all is not well in education. However, little of a dramatic nature has taken place to address this national crisis. The public school system is incapable of reforming itself from within. Governments—local, state and federal—have been ineffective in bringing about meaningful change from the outside. The federal government lacks the political will while state and local governments lack the necessary courage. All levels of government are unwilling to take on the powerful teacher unions and vested interest groups. Consequently, the public accepts school failures as an inevitable outcome.

Positioning a District for Change

This book is not just a critique; it proposes seven strategies to make things right, to turn things around, to bring success to all students. The ideas are my own and are based on many years of working in education in multiple capacities. Other observers of public education will have different ideas.

After retiring as superintendent, I worked for fifteen years as a search consultant. I have been employed in numerous states and during those years made professional friends and contacts in many school systems. Many of their experiences and opinions are reflected in this book. I have spent most of my adult life working in schools, learning to be an administrator, and committing a considerable amount of time trying to teach others the art of leadership.

One of the very hard lessons I learned during my career as a superintendent is that the institutions that represent us do not take kindly to those of us who disagree with an organizational position. Consequently, those superintendents with challenging ideas are either pressured into marching in lockstep with the leadership or being locked out of the organization's inner circles. It is not surprising that educational organizations have squelched individual thought, independent thinking, and creative dissent. Baseball is not the only venue where the battle cry is "play ball!"

Learning to Survive a School

I believe that no children should be exposed to schools that have little regard for them. I speak from experience in that, in some ways, I am a product of such a school. I attended a small urban high school and cannot think of a single teacher who cared much whether I learned anything or not. Not one could have been described as inspiring or motivational. The school was a nice old-boy institution where students who were doing well received the most attention and those who were struggling, as I was, had no place to go for help. Most of the skill I achieved in English and in writing, the basic underpinning of all education, was acquired in college and in army intelligence school.

I remember as though it was yesterday the day during my senior year in high school when my guidance counselor informed me I would be better suited to working in one of the paper mills in the city rather than attending college. At age seventeen, I was sufficiently street smart to understand that he was one of the marginally competent educators I frequently reference in this book. I took a pass on his guidance. Over the years I have occasionally wondered how this counselor would react if he knew that I acquired my undergraduate degree with honors, went on to earn two graduate degrees, and held a position in education that could have made him my employee.

If ignoring my academic needs was not a sufficient blow to my self-esteem, there was the question of ethnic prejudice that I frequently experienced both in school and on the athletic field. I survived this school and learned valuable lessons that helped guide my career and that remain with me today. But no student anywhere should have to learn how to "survive" a school. This book is about educators guaranteeing that students thrive, not just survive.

Acknowledgments

TO RUTH FOR EVERYTHING, BUT ESPECIALLY for her belief in and support of my work. Thanks to two educators who reviewed an early draft of the manuscript. Both reacted positively to the manuscript, but that should not be taken to mean they agreed with all of the material. To Russell F. Farnen, of Farmington, Connecticut, professor of political science, the author of numerous college texts and former director of the University of Connecticut, Hartford Regional Campus, in West Hartford, Connecticut, who gave so generously of his time and who provided many key ideas for reorganization of the materials and whose edits were of great help. To Dr. Doris Kurtz, superintendent of schools in New Britain, Connecticut. Her edits of the first draft of this manuscript resulted in numerous changes and improvements. She brought to the review process the perspective of an urban school system and emphasized to the author the important roles that athletics and parent involvement play in the lives of urban students. Dr. Kurtz is the "strong" leader type mentioned in a positive way in the book.

Special thanks to the nine readers of the final draft. Their various perspectives resulted in many new ideas being included and original ones modified. Their unanimous positive reaction to the final draft should not be taken to mean that they agreed with everything proposed by the author.

Mrs. Joanne Beers, parent of a high school student and president of the Avon Educational Foundation, Avon, Connecticut.

Dr. Michael Buckley, Associate Executive Director, and Director of the Connecticut Principals' Academy, Connecticut Association of Schools.

Dr. Mark Cohan, Superintendent of Schools, Norwich Free Academy, Norwich, Connecticut.

Ms. Pamela Gourlie, former chairperson of the East Haddam Board of Education, East Haddam, Connecticut.

Mr. Monte Hopper, former chairperson of the Avon Board of Education, Avon, Connecticut.

Dr. Margaret O. Killinger, Rezendes Preceptor for the Arts, Honors College, University of Maine at Orono, and author of *The Good Life of Helen K. Nearing.*

Dr. Frances Rabinowitz, Superintendent of Schools, Hamden, Connecticut, formerly Associate Commissioner of Education for Teaching and Learning, Certification, Support and Assessment, Connecticut Department of Education, Hartford, Connecticut.

Dr. Greg Riccio, Superintendent of Schools, Nadaburg Unified School District No. 81, Nadaburg, Arizona, and a former high school principal.

Ms. Patricia Smith, retired intermediate school principal, Avon, Connecticut.

Introduction: A Different Perspective

Abandonment of Students

E DUCATIONAL LEADERS HAVE ABANDONED large numbers of students in their quest for academic success. They failed to design the educational enterprise in a way that all students are able to achieve at high levels. I suggest that these same leaders have squandered billions of dollars on curriculum materials, new programs, marginal employees, and irrelevant professional staff development activities that have had little or no positive impact on student learning. As a result, the majority of our schools are neither outstanding nor highly competitive and many students attend these schools unchallenged and unsuccessful. Because of this extraordinary and continuing failure, our schools place our children at risk of failing in school; they place the nation at risk of losing untapped genius.

Shouldering Responsibility

The responsibility for this state of affairs rests squarely on the shoulders of those who are elected to lead and those who are paid to lead, namely: board of education members, school superintendents, state departments of education, and legislative bodies. The reason for this state of affairs is a perspective issue: the inability of the two most influential players in education—boards of education and superintendents—to accept alternative ways of conducting

xviii   *Introduction: A Different Perspective*

business; and their failure to mobilize others to advocate for successful schools.

Our schools are funded by taxpayers; therefore, boards of education and superintendents manage schools with someone else's money. Once they deplete the funds they have been provided, they almost always request more and are offended when more is not forthcoming. When additional funds are not forthcoming, boards and superintendents often point fingers at those they erroneously believe are the cause; namely, the old, the retired, the empty nesters, the taxpayers association, those disgruntled over the quality of schooling, and unsuccessful adults who attended these or other failing schools as children. Educational leaders lean towards believing that these groups want to reduce budgets for selfish reasons, or that they are simply out of touch with the way schools operate and the need for annual infusions of new funds.

What these leaders do not accept is the fact that there are citizens, young and old, those without children and many with children, those with students in school and those with children yet to enter school, who simply are unable to fund schools at the level that educators desire. By playing the blame game, boards and superintendents are often successful at insulating themselves from the consequences of unsuccessful schools. It is all too easy to blame someone else, to have someone else shoulder the failings of public schools.

A Different Perspective

If we are to have any chance to dramatically improve instruction and student achievement, to make our schools successful for all students, a board and its superintendent must adopt a different perspective and a new strategy, one in which they:

- Assume they own the school system
- Invest their own risk capital
- Operate it as an entrepreneurial enterprise
- Measure "profits" in terms of improved student achievement
- Develop creative ways to live with either level or diminishing resources
- Guarantee that all students (customers) will learn at high levels
- Be prepared to be "shuttered" if their enterprise is not successful

Boards of education and school superintendents must cease thinking they are a not-for-profit business and begin acting like a free-market enterprise. They must operate schools as though it is their money that is being expended, not someone else's. They must accept the fact that unless they meet the mandate of producing a smarter, higher-achieving student with the resources provided to them, the school district has little reason to exist as an organization. Educational leadership and board leadership must be something more than asking for more.

Prologue

"What time do you have to leave?"

"Around 12:30. That will get me there in time to hear the guest speaker, around 1:30."

"You usually don't attend these meetings of state superintendents now that you are retired. Is something special going on?"

"Yes, the speaker will be sharing his strategies for improving our schools. They are the strategies he has made the focus of his new book, *A Power Shift in Public Education.*"

"Who says schools need improvement? The last time I looked, our schools were receiving rave reviews from parents who thought test scores were outstanding."

"You can't judge success or failure of schools nationally by our schools. Not all schools have the leadership, the quality of personnel, or the finances to be successful. It is a fact that communities with deep pockets are better able to be successful."

"Can you give me an example?"

"Sure, the wealthy suburbs are more apt to have board of education members who are well educated themselves. They would understand the need for education, are supportive of a strong school program, and live in a community with the money to make it happen. Not every community has these resources. Only a small fraction of school systems in the nation have deep pockets."

"Give me another example of the ideas this speaker is sharing with the superintendents."

"I have to assume that he will deal with the issue of taxpayers' revolt against the salaries and benefits that teachers receive. It is an issue that never goes away."

"Not only are those who are revolting not going away, they are growing stronger by the day. I can understand why he would address it."

"I'd also have to think that he will discuss superintendent leadership styles since this is a group of superintendents. But the fact is I know little more than you do. I only know that the e-mail announcing his speaking engagement mentioned that he had strategies which, if implemented by a school district, will guarantee a greater level of success for students. From reading between the lines, several of them are controversial and may stir up those in attendance. Now that I think of it, the subtitle to the book is *Strategies for Dealing with Broken Promises.*"

"It doesn't appear that the association has provided much information about him."

"I think that may be by design. It sent just enough data to pique one's interest. It will keep the members interested and will almost guarantee a big audience."

"Were there any other hints in the e-mail?"

"Well, there was an offhanded reference about boards of education. Given the theme of the book, a power shift, it has to refer to boards of education needing to exert greater power. The fact is that his strategies will be controversial, otherwise he would not have been invited to speak to this group."

"For whom would his strategies be controversial? I thought you said that the idea behind the book was to improve education. Why would that be controversial to educators?"

"When we mention superintendents, we are talking about one of the most conservative groups in the county, which is why education in general is not forward looking. Any movement from the status quo will most likely be seen as a challenge to the 'business as usual' environment that educators desire. That may sound critical, but it is not. Just an historical fact."

"You were part of that scene for decades. Is this the way you would react? I can't believe you would."

"Rather than look at my experience, it is more profitable to examine the profession as a whole. How conservative you will be would depend upon where you are in your career. In the early years, you want change and are bored to death without it. In mid-career, you begin to become a bit cautious, partly because you are tired of the constant pressure and what you see as unappreciative constituents."

"How about at the end of one's career?"

"I think many educators at the end of their careers are tired and simply wish to coast into retirement. At this stage, they want to avoid being hassled. Sometimes, you wish you could be invisible. If younger superintendents are not careful, they could become despondent listening to older superintendents. It is the type of conversation you hear all too often at meetings. The older superintendents spend an inordinate amount of time discussing and computing their pension benefits, deferred income, travel and retirement plans. It is unfortunate because this is the time in your career when you know so much, have little to lose, and are generally respected enough to be listened to. Major changes would be relatively easy to implement by experienced superintendents."

"So you think that this guy is going to beat up on superintendents?"

"No, but I do assume that he will challenge them, and test their tolerance for a shift in power. Again, I do not know the speaker so whatever I am telling you is pure conjecture."

"Anyone else in his line of fire?"

"As I said, I have no idea about the strategies in the book, what they are, or who they are directed at except for that one comment about boards of education."

"Any ideas as to the overall theme of his strategies?"

"I think he will refer to the need to make major changes, changes that will create movement and energy. The strategies are probably designed to move education in general from a state of inertia to one of action. And, the truth is that we need a major shift in doing business. Education across the nation has been a dismal failure for millions of students. The national dropout rate is a national disaster, a disgrace at best. Even in this rich state, the dropout rate in urban schools is alarming. It is time for a new effort since the old one is unsuccessful. "

"Are you concerned about the reaction to his comments?"

"Not really. There will be some angst, but no one at the meeting should be concerned about an effort to improve student success. It is an issue that should be raised continuously. Public education is in trouble and the old model needs to be replaced. A power shift may be the answer. I'm hoping his speech will have a positive thrust."

"Will you engage this guy in conversation? You usually challenge the ideas of others. I know you do this to spark interest but that is not the way it always comes across."

"I plan on being a careful listener because I am really interested in new ideas that could lead to student success. I am no longer active, but I am still interested in successful schools. Besides, the guy deserves the right to be heard. Those of us in the audience should be pleased that he is willing to share his strategies before a potentially critical audience. No, I want him to have the opportunity to share ideas that could lead to more successful schools."

"What time will you be home?"

"Late afternoon, certainly in time for happy hour. Why?"

"I want to hear what he had to say. Educators are not the only ones interested in addressing the issue of failing schools. When schools are not successful, the taxpayer, me, ends up paying for the solutions, most of which never work. All parents should have a high level of interest in making schools better for their children. I'll be anxious to hear what he said and the audience reaction to it. So, I'll be waiting."

1

Unsuccessful Schools Threaten
Our Nation

The Role of Public Education

THE NEED TO DRAMATICALLY IMPROVE free public education for all students is of the highest priority for our society and it remains the primary goal of the elementary and secondary school system. Often forgotten in our quest for excellence is the fact that the physical and political survival of our nation was one of the reasons why we adopted the then-unheard-of concept of a free, public education.

Our forefathers understood the threat that an illiterate population posed for the future of the nation. They knew that the country could not continue to defend itself with citizen militias bearing rifles and pitchforks. To survive as a nation, we needed an educated citizenry. An enlightened citizenry would be the result of public schools that provided free education for all. Once that concept was ingrained in the thinking of our leaders, our schools and the survival of a nation were forever entwined. Neither can survive without the other. This book is about the survival of both.

Who Represents the People

Given the current economic and military threat to our country from emerging and developing nations around the world, and the manner in which the United States Congress for several decades has ignored what is in the best interests of the citizens it represents, our survival now is as much at risk as it was at the time of the founding of the nation. This is a government that over several decades and both administrations created the energy crisis, the credit crisis, and national debt crisis. It is a government that appears to have engaged the country in the Iraq war based on fictitious and deceitful data, and has mismanaged the occupation. It has become adept at creating enemies faster than the armed forces can eliminate them. It has crippled our intelligence services, created national unrest, impoverished many of its citizens, and manipulated loopholes in our laws to hide its many misdeeds. The failure of the government to oversee its most important institutions has brought the country to its knees.

Because of these failures, many citizens question the quality of their future. One cannot help but wonder if the concept of a senate as one arm of Congress is an outmoded concept given its record of failing to provide for its citizens. Is it possible for 100 of the most powerful individuals on the face of the earth to understand and be guardians of our future? Has the Senate become a club of millionaires and billionaires? And, if so, is it reasonable to believe that its members can truly appreciate the plight of the average American? Is there a better method for representing the will of the people? Is a senate that is controlled by lobbyists and special interest groups serving the citizenry in the manner that our forefathers anticipated?

The more critical question is whether the full Congress is capable of strengthening our nation's schools. These are questions that need answers. Only time will tell if the new administration is capable of providing the leadership needed to rebuild government so that it represents all of its citizens and is able to secure a safe and prosperous future for the nation. This is the hope of both the majority of Americans who voted for the Obama administration and most of those who did not. The question is whether the new secretary of education is too moderate to bring about significant change.

Our Leadership As a Nation Is Challenged

When the United States was founded, there were but a handful of nations with whom we had to compete economically, educationally, and against whom we had to defend ourselves militarily. For the last 100 years we have been the greatest economic and military power on the face of the planet. Our public school system was the envy of the free world. This is no longer true. Today, we face numerous nations with more powerful economies than ours and several nations with a growing military capability that challenges our own diminishing superiority.

Many nations now produce students who challenge ours at every level of the educational ladder but none more so than at the graduate level. Many of these same nations have developed school systems far more advanced than ours, and their students are more highly challenged and motivated to succeed. We only need to look at the outstanding academic success rate of Asian and Indian students whose families have immigrated to our country in order to realize that native-born students have failed to achieve at the highest levels.

Foreign students dominate our graduate schools in science and mathematics. Our colleges and universities have bred generations of coddled, binge-drinking, undisciplined adolescents unprepared for the highly competitive world they live in. Rather than educate large numbers of future political and business leaders, our colleges and universities have graduated pampered conformists and followers.

Our National Leaders Have Failed Us

We have failed as a nation to develop political leaders who place the good of the nation ahead of their personal and political ambitions. Consequently, we now find ourselves:

- Diminished as a world power
- Hated by adversaries around the globe
- Held hostage by countries that control energy sources
- Distrusted by friendly nations
- Divided at home through our poisonous political process, a process that is manipulated by powerful special interest groups and lobbyists

Furthermore, our banking and investment institutions have unleashed the greatest threat to our economic health since the Great Depression, and our stature as a world power—educationally, politically, militarily, and economically—has been severely damaged by those in power whether they be in politics, business, or education.

Our future as a superpower, capable of caring for all its citizens economically and militarily, is questionable unless there is a major change in the way we educate our students and the manner in which we support the most gifted among them. Without a dramatic improvement in the success rate for all students, and a major leap in the achievement level for our most talented students, we will continue to witness the decline of our nation.

The stakes are high, and our Congress and recent administrations have demonstrated little or no resolve in addressing national problems that threaten our nation and our schools. Congressional rules allow one or two powerful committee chairpersons or the leaders of the House and Senate to hold hostage legislation that would benefit the nation. These individuals place party loyalty above the general good.

It took decades for the Department of Education in Washington to pass the No Child Left Behind Act, and then Congress failed to adequately fund it. Nationally, there is no articulated goal to identify those areas of our economy that are threatened and to then underwrite, directly or indirectly, the cost of educating students needed in those specialties that would strengthen the nation. The Department of Education has a long history of failing to gain the respect of the educational community.

State and Local Leaders Are Misguided

At the state level, educators and legislators have placed far too much emphasis on magnet schools as the primary solution to educate underperforming urban students and as a way to resolve racial isolation. While there may be instances where some states coordinate their magnet school efforts, there is no national agenda to coordinate the offerings of magnet schools in order to address national needs. Each state operates as an entity unto itself with little regard for the national economy.

Magnet schools, rather than improve secondary education for all students, simply extract the most talented or motivated students out of comprehensive high schools and bundle them together in an educational arrangement where the students have the newest facilities, the most talented teachers, and substantial resources. Meanwhile, the local comprehensive high school is starved for basic necessities. If in fact the comprehensive high school is an outmoded system of education, as suggested by some educators, then the answer is not to select a few to attend magnet or other specialty schools; the answer is to provide an alternative system of education for every child without exception.

Like other areas in our economy wherein special people receive special treatment, magnet schools are the beginning of the "have and have not" mentality in public schools. It is a scheme that is contrary to the democratic purpose of free public education for all. Unless all students have the same benefits as those attending magnet schools or all students have the opportunity to attend magnet schools, we will end up with a two-tiered education system. It is encouraging to see the Hartford, Connecticut, public schools creating numerous specialty high schools. The goal must be to place all students in the city in a setting in which they can succeed, otherwise magnet schools create the same type of discrimination in schooling that they were intended to eliminate!

One cannot help but be bewildered when one hears educators condemning comprehensive high schools for their inability to educate students when it has been the educational leadership that has brought these schools to their knees. The lack of funding and the creation of charter schools and magnet schools siphon off the resources so badly needed by comprehensive high schools. The irony is that on one hand superintendents strip the comprehensive high school of the means for success and bemoan the fact that these same schools fail. Then the failure is used to justify still another magnet school.

Meanwhile, at the local level, boards of education remain mired in minutiae, using precious time to debate inconsequential matters and expending funds on programs that have little return. Consistent with our history, educational leaders spend much time solving problems of their own making.

Lack of Student Success

It is somewhat interesting that in my home state (no doubt similar to other states) educators at the local and state level compliment one another when there is a slight improvement in the results of the state's testing program. What they fail to emphasize to the taxpayer is that the test measures "proficiency," the lowest level of "passing." This is the best the state can claim after decades of efforts that cost the taxpayers millions of dollars. This lack of achievement occurs in a state considered well above the average in the nation for schooling and certainly for wealth. What then are the achievement levels in states that score below the average and what does it mean for the future of our nation when untold numbers of students cannot read or write at proficiency levels?

It is clear that the goal of dramatically improving student performance is of paramount importance if the United States is to survive as a strong and viable society that will breed the next generation of leaders in education, government, business, and the sciences, including technology and medicine. Without excellence in our schools, and without the ability to compete intellectually with other nations in all arenas, our country runs the risk of becoming a third-world society among the industrialized nations.

When schools do not measure up to what is demanded of them, corrective action must be taken. The time is past when state departments of education can vacillate in addressing failing school districts. Schools that continually fail students must be shuttered. Transferring marginally competent educators between schools in the same district or one district to another can no longer be an option. Teachers unions, which are partially to blame by protecting marginal teachers, must join forces with state officials in their efforts to put poorly performing schools out of business.

History of Squandering Valuable Resources

Students have but one opportunity to succeed in any given grade or program, and they must not wait years for a school system to restructure. For too long, the elementary and secondary education profession has tolerated the marginally competent and the incompetent at all levels of the organization, from classroom to boardroom.

Any analysis by state and local boards of education as to the reasons schools do not measure up to high standards must not be another incentive for the leadership to authorize still another rewriting of curriculum or to add another new program to those that currently do not work. Schools need to first remove programs that have not been successful in assisting underachieving students. Boards of education and school superintendents need to possess calculators that have a minus function. School administrators have a propensity to add new programs without removing others. It is worth noting that in spite of the fact that curricula are constantly being revised and new ones introduced, students have difficulty reaching proficiency in basic language and mathematical skills. The answer to improving schools is not another new program.

In my opinion, and in an attempt to resolve the issue of nonperforming schools, any analysis must be viewed through the lenses of personnel shortcomings rather than through program and material shortcomings. The reason is simple. There has never been a shortage of curriculum materials developed for use in instructing students in underperforming districts.

Since October 4, 1957, when the launching of the Soviet Union's *Sputnik* stunned the American academic, scientific, technological, and political worlds, educators have written and publishers have created instructional materials to address every conceivable area of instruction. However, significant improvement in achievement levels has not occurred. With *Sputnik*'s successful launch, vast amounts of federal money flowed with ease directly to state departments of education and eventually to local school districts. Colleges and universities were recipients of substantial government grants to be employed to experiment with new programs and approaches to teaching. Hundreds of public schools served as research sites for university research projects. But, some fifty years later, we are still attempting, without much success, to dramatically reform our educational system.

Education has a long history of transitioning from one program to another perhaps in the hope of diverting attention from those that do not work. Whether we speak of advanced placement or remedial courses, and all that exists in between, there is a wealth of materials now available, as has been true for decades.

It is also a fact that there has been an army of highly paid consultants employed throughout the country working with local districts in an effort to improve underperforming schools. This is especially true in many large urban districts where generous government grants and corporate gift giving have made funding for materials, programs, and consultants readily available. There is not one area of education for which "experts" have not been employed to seek answers to the fundamental question of why our schools do not perform at high levels.

Tens of millions of dollars have been spent to purchase instructional materials or programs to compensate for ineffective teaching. Nevertheless, one-third of the schools in Connecticut, at the time of this writing one of the highest-rated school systems in the nation, did not reach proficiency. It is projected that this number will grow. The reason is obvious: reform efforts, for the most part, have addressed curriculum design and curriculum materials, and have avoided addressing the shortcomings of teachers, administrators, and boards of education.

Efforts at Reform

Not to be lost in a maze of new materials and programs is the fact that many educational and philanthropic institutions have attempted to reform high schools. The motivation for several of these reforms grew out of the early work of Ted Sizer and Brown University with its Coalition of Essential Schools project. In spite of individual successes with the coalition initiatives and those of other prominent institutions at the national and state level, no project has been able to replicate successes of participating high schools in large numbers; successes have been isolated.

It is impossible to list the hundreds if not thousands of efforts and programs designed to improve the work of superintendents and administrators. Still, many of our schools are not performing at high levels.

Citizens and taxpayers have given new programs, curriculum redesign, and special projects more than ample time to work. Now, successful school reform will only come about if it is people driven and not program driven. All districts, especially underperforming districts and schools, must commit themselves to adopting new strategies which, if fully implemented, will help drive a district to academic excellence for all students.

Although it is naïve to believe that all students will achieve at the highest level, school systems must still establish high standards and commit themselves to moving all students to those heights while recognizing the limitations of a certain percentage of the student population. If a district desires to join the ranks of successful schools across the nation, and if it wants to drive its system to new academic heights, then it must commit itself to adopting seven strategies that are directed at improving student achievement. Based on forty years in education as a teacher, coach, administrator, superintendent, search consultant, and general consultant, I have identified seven strategies that have the power to propel school systems to greater success. They are:

- A board of education that uses its authority to bring about change
- Academic leadership provided by the superintendent of schools
- Instructional power at the building level
- A powerful and equitable recruiting system
- Staffing levels appropriate to the challenge
- Tenure track–performance track options for teachers
- Performance-based compensation for superintendents

These strategies have the potential to transform underperforming schools into successful schools. They have the potential to motivate successful schools to new academic heights. The degree to which any of the strategies are missing, poorly implemented, or otherwise deficient is the degree to which the school system is incapable of internal reform and, therefore, unable to be successful in serving all of its students.

The obstacle to transforming an underperforming school system into a successful school system is a board of education that allows low standards to become institutionalized. Once a district begins its slide into mediocrity, full recovery is next to impossible and the opportunity or chance of becoming a successful school district is lost. When the majority of school districts in the nation cannot enter the world of successful schools, the nation is at risk.

What Needs to Be Done

This book is about what we need to do if we expect students—all students—to learn at the highest level. It is about making every school successful for every child who passes through its doors. For many decades, the profession used as an excuse for poor classroom performance the fact that teachers were underpaid and overworked, making it difficult to recruit and retain outstanding teachers. The same argument was made for administrators. This is no longer the case. Consider the following:

- Educators at all levels of the organization are now paid competitive wages.
- They are provided with extensive holiday/vacation periods, which have a significant monetary value.
- They enjoy fringe benefits and pensions that exceed those offered in the private sector for equivalent job responsibilities.
- They have contracts that guarantee a well-defined work schedule.
- They have a positive work environment.
- Unlike those who work in the private sector and who are continually faced with being downsized, educators with the most minimal of competencies enjoy what amounts to lifetime employment and generous retirement benefits.

Powerful teachers unions have resisted most efforts to make it easier for districts to terminate some tenured teachers who are at best just marginal performers. These same unions have outwitted boards of education across the country by making compensation restricted to the single-salary schedule, which does not differentiate pay based on competency. What economic madness it is that a compensation system provides the least competent the same compensation as the most competent! It is a system that makes it difficult to attract outstanding individuals to education and it squanders taxpayer money.

In spite of the vast financial resources that have been provided to local boards of education, school administrators, and teachers, as a group they have not provided the improvement in achievement that was expected. Many have managed to institutionalize mediocrity. Schools are simply not as successful as they need to be.

To understand how far we have fallen in our educational institutions, we need only look to the number of engineers, physicists, doctors, researchers, and other professionals who have immigrated to our country from what we used to think of as third-world countries to fill positions that are beyond the ability of our college and university graduates. Our nation's schools have been severely damaged by bad leaders who have given us bad schools. Bad schools undermine the foundation of our nation.

Key Chapter 1 Ideas

The United States Congress has not served the best interests of its citizens.
The government has placed the nation at risk.
Many nations now challenge us in every arena.
The Bush administration has created adversaries around the globe.

Formerly friendly nations are distrustful of us.

Our status as a superpower is challenged.

Educators have undermined the comprehensive high school.

Our students at all levels are being outperformed by those of other nations.

Fifty years after *Sputnik* we still seek educational reform.

Powerful teachers unions inhibit the development of successful schools.

It is time to adopt the strategies necessary for academic excellence.

2

Strategy Number 1: Power at the Top

A Dedicated, Creative, and Competent Board of Education

THE BOARD OF EDUCATION IS THE SINGLE most important strategy in a district's quest to dramatically improve the quality of education in its schools. To be effective, it must demonstrate dedication, creativity, and competence. It must operate at the highest moral and ethical standards. It needs to develop the energy and excitement that motivates the staff to perform at the highest levels. It needs to create an environment that makes employees proud that they work in the district. It must articulate clearly and precisely the necessary educational outcomes for the district. Finally, a board must keep its eye on the academic target. The board, positioned at the top of the authority hierarchy, is responsible for the failures of all others who work in the district.

The idea that a powerful board of education is the most important strategy in a district's drive towards excellence for all students will come as something of a surprise, perhaps dismay, to school superintendents who have traditionally viewed their work as the most important. This is understandable in that historically the vast majority of boards of education have assumed a role subordinate to strong superintendents. This is a major error in strategy because it is the board that represents the first line of attack in a district's effort to promote excellence. It is the political body in which the public has placed its trust, believing that administrators and staff will educate children at the highest levels of achievement. It is the standard-bearer that leads staff to challenge educational frontiers. It represents a shining example of democracy at work: citizens duly elected to preserve this great nation through its children. Once its members have taken the oath of office, they then represent all the people and must cut their ties to vested interest groups. They have now been entrusted to speak for the children, no greater a calling.

Ironically, a board of education is more often than not seen as a minor player in that its work is considered secondary to that of the superintendent. In many cases dominant superintendents have pushed them into the background. This is unfortunate since, if a board wishes to propel the district forward in a serious quest for excellence, it, coupled with an accomplished superintendent, must be the driving force for change because it is the entity directly responsible to the public. Superintendents are executive directors who implement the directions which the board established; while they may recommend direction, they do not establish direction.

Many will challenge the priority given to this strategy, noting that it is difficult to encourage a sufficient number of citizens to run for office and fill board of education positions. If this is true, it does not diminish the priority assigned to this strategy; it merely points out an associated problem: the political roadblocks placed in the way of good people wanting to run for office. Far too many communities use the political caucus system to "screen those eligible to run for office." Too often they reject those who have a tendency to stray from the party line. If you are an independent thinker, there is no room for you at the inn.

Those who currently serve on boards of education have a responsibility to pave the way in a community for others to serve. If boards of education are viewed to be the primary strategy in a district's drive to have successful schools, and if they are seen as something more than a body that simply rubber-stamps administrative initiatives, it may be that others will serve.

If a board of education is to fulfill its role as the primary strategy necessary to bring success to all of our schools, it must successfully address and successfully complete four goals:

1. Create and initiate big ideas on behalf of students.
2. Develop a powerful and equitable recruitment and retention of staff policy.
3. Be fiscally responsible.
4. Provide objective oversight and evaluation of the superintendent of schools.

Some in the educational community will question why these four goals are highlighted, believing that the first two in particular have long been viewed as the responsibility of the superintendent. The third goal, fiscal responsibility, is often taken as a given, yet it is a goal that is most often neglected. A board of education that manages finances poorly creates a significant level of hostility with the general public. The fourth goal, oversight of the superintendent, will seem to some to be a routine effort of the board and therefore unnecessary to single out as a major concern. Sadly, many boards of education do not do an outstanding job in meeting this goal.

Others will wonder about the absence of goals that address a mission statement, or policy development, or communications. And why is the oversight and evaluation of the superintendent a major goal of a board of education? The answer is that, in my opinion, these four goals, if achieved, will build the essential foundation needed to spur gains in student achievement and the development of successful schools. Subsequent chapters will outline why these four goals are the most important ones if the board is to propel the district forward.

All four goals must be in play simultaneously and they must remain a continuous effort. They are all essential to a smoothly running educational enterprise. When a board engages in a self-evaluation at year's end, these four goals must be utilized as the primary areas of self-evaluation. A board may have other goals it deems important to its success, but none will matter much if they have not successfully addressed these four primary goals. A board should dismiss the use of standardized assessment checklists that deal with many irrelevant and inconsequential matters.

The board of education's quest for excellence is easier stated than accomplished. Mark Twain is reported to have said, "In the first place God made idiots. This was for practice. Then he made school boards." Perhaps he was a bit harsh in his opinion, but as a participant in education for more than forty years, my sense is that there is some element of truth in Twain's observation.

I spent the last fifteen years of my career as an educational search consultant. In addition, I contracted with a number of boards of education on reorganization studies and personnel training. During those years, I was engaged with more than 100 boards of education and an equal number of school superintendents. I concluded that boards are of three types.

Type One

The first, few in number, had as their primary agenda the improvement of education for all students. These boards understood their roles and demonstrated the courage to attack flaws that impeded the drive towards excellence for all students. There was no question in the minds of the individual board members that collectively they were the propellant that energized the district. Three of those outstanding boards with whom I worked exemplify what all boards of education should strive for: to provide educational leadership and initiative and not simply respond to issues brought to them. These boards are forward looking and do not allow short-term matters to impede their efforts.

Interestingly enough, the three communities had differing profiles in terms of economics and demographics. One was rural with a large summer population that hailed from the metropolitan New York area. Another was a blue-collar district that was a Boston, Massachusetts, suburb. The third was an exclusive and wealthy suburb of a metropolitan area. On a scale of 1–10 as it relates to establishing and maintaining a climate in which educational excellence for all students is the norm, these three boards would rate a 9–10. These boards demonstrated that, regardless of size and demographics, excellence in board operations can occur in any district in the nation.

Type Two

The second group of boards were those that struggled to achieve a rating of 5 on a 1–10 scale. They all shared two similar traits: first, they employed leaders who did not possess the qualifications to propel the district to excellence; and second, board members were not engaged in developing "big ideas" to improve education in their district. Rather, they were bogged down with details that better belonged to central office personnel.

In all cases, the board was not in the driver's seat. Board members in these districts rarely attended the training sessions that their state associations offered, and most members declined offers to join their own staff in professional training at home. They usually focused on narrow, mundane issues. Consequently, they tended to employ superintendents who shared those same values and, by doing so, set the stage for mediocrity. They were essentially journeyman board members who employed journeyman superintendents. They led districts that will not appear on the radar screen if one is scanning the educational universe for excellence. They are best described as plain vanilla, generic brand school systems.

Type Three

The third group of boards created turmoil in their districts. The interests of individual board members almost always were selfish, using the system to create favorable conditions for their relatives, promoting and hiring candidates to satisfy political promises, or starving the system of the services of highly competent professional educators from outside the system and engaging in political appointments and favoritism within. They tended to ignore ethical hiring practices and viewed promotion of those who are politically connected as the correct way to conduct business. With regularity, these districts failed students.

Setting the Tone for the District

In most districts, the board of education, the teaching and administrative staffs, and the public rely on the superintendent to establish the tone for the school system. This occurs when boards of education remain silent or invisible. A board should be considered derelict in its duties and responsibility if it fails to set the standards that a district must follow. At the same time, a board is professionally remiss if, in setting standards, it sets standards that fail to promote excellence. A board of education must create the cultural, ethical, and educational yardsticks in a district and must not delegate this responsibility to the superintendent of schools. If the latter occurs, then the superintendent assumes the role of the board and the board loses sight of its obligations.

In addition to setting district standards of performance, a successful board of education models personal behavior and process to the staff and community. A board cannot expect outstanding work and professional conduct from those it employs unless individual board members display those behaviors for them. Respect for others begins with the board.

It is unrealistic for a community to believe that it can achieve an outstanding school system without an outstanding board of education. For this reason alone, voters need to take a great interest in those they elect to a board of education. It is actually at the moment of voting in a school district that a community decides if its schools will achieve outstanding success. A community should expect from its schools no more than the investment it made during elections.

Assuming that the voters elected those who are well intended, what then is a board of education to do if it wishes to develop an outstanding school system? How does it build energy, power, and initiatives into the system? What are the essential ingredients that must be in the mix if it is to compete with the most outstanding and powerful districts in the nation? Is it possible to move a district from being mediocre, a nonplayer, to being highly competitive? The answer is both yes and no. It will depend upon the level of courage a board possesses in attacking big issues and how competent it is in designing systems that build strength. It will depend upon their choice of superintendent of schools. The mantra is that if a board hires a superintendent with average ability, it can expect to achieve average results. When it employs an outstanding educational leader, it can expect exceptional results. If it makes a political appointment, it can expect political results.

Based on many years of being the superintendent in a successful school district and working in over 100 other districts as a search consultant and general consultant, I have identified what to me are the four most critical goals that need to be addressed by a board of education if it is to be considered the most important of the seven strategies in a drive to develop an outstanding school system. Each of the next four chapters addresses one of the four goals.

Key Chapter 2 Ideas

The board of education is the single most powerful strategy to success.
Historically, boards have been viewed as subordinate to the superintendent.
Communities need to elect competent citizens to the board.
Incumbent members must help recruit their replacements.
The successful board has four major goals to accomplish.
Boards of education generally fall into three governing types.
A board of education must appoint or elect an outstanding superintendent.

3

Create and Initiate "Big Ideas"

Big Ideas

MEMBERS OF A BOARD OF EDUCATION must have, collectively, a vision of what education must be if it is to serve all students. Such a board will establish the "big ideas" for the district and drive the district to accomplish its goals. It must not allow short-term issues to distract it from undertaking major initiatives.

The most effective board I worked with had the big idea that it could provide a far better educational product than it had been delivering; therefore, it set its sights on thinking big. The board decided that it would rid itself of the "generic brand" label it possessed as a school system and make a major move to be highly competitive, to create a system in which all students can succeed, to appear on the national radar screen with other successful systems. Their big idea was embedded in three efforts: improving academic achievement across the system in order that the district would be competitive with the best in the nation; addressing the needs of all children with emphasis on those who may otherwise be neglected; embedding the notion of "the whole child" into the district culture. This was a three-part big idea. Every district will individualize its big ideas to meet its needs. This particular big idea was simple in its goal, but was so powerful a statement that it remained the mantra for the district for many years.

Some boards have the ability to identify big ideas for a district without any outside assistance. Others may need to employ a consultant to assist it in identifying big ideas. If a board does decide to employ a consultant, it must use caution and not allow itself to become entangled in complex design systems that require constant oversight.

A colleague has suggested that the department of education in a given state create its own big ideas for local communities in the absence of action by a local board of education. While that may be more efficient, the danger in having big ideas created too far from local control is that they would not reflect what is needed in a community.

Trying to provide oversight in an era when there is a general shortage of administrators in school districts is often the death knell for strategic plans or complex systems. Such plans tend to overwhelm the participants once the excitement and camaraderie of the planning sessions come to an end. As the months go on and targets are not met, the afterglow quickly fades. Another reason complex plans often fail is that elections bring new members to the board who have no shared ownership of the long-range plan. Some new members may have run for office because they were opposed to the plan.

It is vital for a board to be mindful that a big idea does not infer a complex design. The idea itself may be simple in its goal, but its implementation requires a realistic board commitment to make things right for children. My experience is such that I believe that most boards have the ability to establish big ideas. However, they often fail to use their authority and power to make the correct professional decisions. Whenever a board initiates a major change, it is not without some pain, as will be noted later in this section.

Diverse Board Membership

When a board has a membership that thinks alike, it has more difficulty in engaging in meaningful debate and in making powerful educational decisions. Alternatively, when a board has a membership that is diverse and that represents different ways of thinking and problem solving, and brings different values to the table, it is more likely to be creative and innovative. Without risk takers and innovators, a board lacks a catalyst for change.

The board mentioned earlier that possessed a mantra that lasted for many years was diverse in its membership. After considerable thought and debate, it was able to create a collective, unified vision for the district. That board was comprised of an engineer, an agronomist, a college administrator, a small contractor, a dentist, an insurance executive, a state representative who was a former English teacher, a homemaker, and a college professor. The age continuum was between thirty-five and sixty-five. It was also a strong board in that it did not allow any town agency or political body to influence its decision to create and implement its big idea.

It is well known that it is the superintendent who is on the front line initiating the will of the board and taking the body blows from constituents, both in and out of the schools. However, it is the board that must exhibit political stamina and have the strength to withstand the unrelenting pressure that undoubtedly will come from most constituents, including unions, politicians, parents, and other taxpayers.

Still another threat to innovation could come from within if employment conditions or changes in traditional work patterns are altered. Whether a board is in a rural community, suburb, or urban setting, there will always be some level of "inbreeding" between members of the administrative and teaching staffs and board members. Consequently, some board members will be pressured when their own administrators and staff want to keep the status quo.

It is also likely that some members of the teacher and administrator ranks will be related to powerful politicians and others of influence in the community. They will use those connections in an effort to halt change. Make no mistake about it, a board with vision must have the courage of its conviction and a collective will if it is to move a district from inertia to initiative.

The Price of Change

Change is also expensive in terms of effort, time, and funding. Implementing big ideas often requires:

- Changes in evaluation and supervision protocols
- Revisions to programs that are not effective
- Termination of traditional programs
- Rejection of initiatives from small but vocal and often hostile vested interest groups
- Opposition from various booster clubs that have ideas of their own that may be compromised by board ideas
- Redeployment and replacement of personnel
- Dismantling of old alliances
- Power shifts within the administrative staff

These are but some of the concerns that a board must weigh when bringing about change. It must never underestimate the opposition. The board must deliberate about the worst case scenario, how it will respond, and the price it may have to pay. It must also maintain the highest ethical standards in order not to give the opposition any cause to distrust the board. Individual members must excuse themselves from any vote if they are in any way compromised by participating in such vote.

Board members are not unlike the citizens they represent. They come from all walks of life. Like any citizen, they have families, businesses, friends, and many have children in school. In addition to those roles, as important as they are, each board member must first be a visionary. They need to understand that their schools have the mission to successfully meet the needs of all students. The measure of a board's success will be documented evidence of improved student achievement.

Board members with big ideas understand another truth: the future success of their schools can be achieved only if they take dramatic action today. In so many ways, "the future is now." The creation of big ideas must not be left to the next board or next election. Once a citizen takes a seat on the board, he or she is now committed to children. There is no other constituency! Governance of the community is left to the legislative branch, finances are left to a fiscal authority. Education is the responsibility of the board of education.

A governing board will be judged first by its actions in propelling a district to excellence; that is, its "big idea." If a board of education is not successful in fulfilling its responsibilities, the school system will not be successful. A board will also be judged on its ability to position itself such that it will stand firm in the face of opponents who would undermine public education in order to satisfy an agenda that is not in the best interest of all students.

Key Chapter 3 Ideas

A board of education must develop "big ideas."

Big ideas need not be complex but must be directed at improving student achievement.

A board with a diverse membership is apt to be more creative and innovative.

With big ideas, a board must expect substantial opposition.

For every board of education, the future is now.

4

Develop a Powerful and Equitable Recruitment Policy

The Critical Importance of Recruiting

THE SECOND MOST IMPORTANT GOAL for a board of education in developing an outstanding school system is a powerful and equitable employee recruiting program. This function is so vital that, in my opinion, if a superintendent were limited to performing a single task, it would have to be that of taking charge of the recruiting process. The road to educational success begins with recruiting.

The underlying philosophy as to why a district must have an effective recruiting program should be self-evident. Staff development, personnel evaluation, and supervision programs are designed to improve upon an employee's qualifications, not develop them. What is missing in a person's essential qualifications at the time of hiring will not be developed once the candidate is employed.

If a school system wishes to squander public funds, an excellent way to do so would be to allow its administrators to attempt to develop a competent teacher out of an incompetent one or an outstanding teacher out of an average one! It simply will not work, and yet that is exactly what most districts attempt to do. It is an effective way to waste valuable financial and human resources.

Districts must be totally committed to hiring outstanding employees. Without an academically powerful and talented teaching and administrative cadre, there is no possibility of building an energized school enterprise that is capable of addressing the needs of all students. Successful school systems are built on the work of successful teachers and administrators.

The Most Vital Rule in Hiring

There is one vital rule that must always be observed in hiring. It is that every person who is employed in a given department or grade must bring talent that is superior to that of the most talented and qualified employee in that department or grade. If this is not accomplished, the system is unable to raise the level of staff competence. Conversely, if your most recent hire is less talented than your best employee, by definition you diminish the average quality of the staff. It is a simple equation that is often ignored when those in charge of school district hiring do their work. Every single person hired must possess talents exceeding that of your most gifted teacher or administrator. A district that adheres to this philosophy is committed to becoming a lighthouse district.

Is such a rule or goal always attainable? Of course it isn't, but if a school system does not use such a standard, it will then settle for something far less. A district owes it to all students to place only the most talented teachers in classrooms. Staffing a school with "warm bodies" does not meet the standard. One cannot calculate the damage inflicted daily upon hundreds of thousands of unsuspecting students when marginally competent teachers and administrators are employed. The reason these employees are hired in the first place is because too often recruiting is delegated to central office administrators who have never taught in a regular classroom or never managed a building. They have not been a colleague of either an outstanding teacher or a poor teacher. They have never been in a classroom to experience the difference between a great class and poor one; they lack the experience that provides a basis of comparison.

As a result of a marginal recruiting system, superintendents often find themselves making demands of teachers and administrators who simply do not possess the ability to perform at a level that guarantees student success! If you employ a plow horse, you cannot plan on receiving a thoroughbred performance. When marginal performers are employed, a district diverts funds and human resources into efforts to solve a problem of its own making and one that is usually without solution other than eventually terminating the employees. While futile attempts are being made to assist those teachers and administrators who are beyond help, students continue to suffer untold damage.

Recruiting Policy

Every district must possess a comprehensive recruiting policy with detailed administrative regulations. The policy and regulations must provide substantial protection to a superintendent and his staff as they build a powerful recruiting system. A superintendent must be willing to guarantee that every candidate, both from inside and outside the school district, has equal access to an open or new position.

In developing a recruiting process for the district, the following are essential components:

- A comprehensive board policy on hiring that also contains language describing the district's expectations as it relates to student learning
- Adherence to all union contract provisions
- Administrative regulations that outline each step of the recruiting process, including a written description of the positions to be filled, the qualifications and experience required, the process for initial paper selection of candidates, and documentation for each step through to the signing of a contract of employment
- Safeguards designed to prevent outside or inside political interference with the hiring process
- Logs of all contacts between any person who has a role in the recruiting program and those who have made contact with this person on behalf of a candidate
- Contacts being defined as personal discussion, telephone calls, e-mail, and any and all electronic or voice messaging systems
- Records of contacts between board members and any member of the school community involved in the hiring process as they pertain to a current or future candidate
- Administrators, board members, interviewers, or others involved in the process must establish a firewall to prevent favoritism in the choice of a candidate
- A safeguard to assure that those in charge of hiring do not favor spouses or relatives of other administrators both in and out of the system
- A prohibition to the eliciting of applications from outside the district when the administration plans on filling from inside the district
- A rule against posting positions with a stringent timetable that makes it impossible for those outside the system to learn of and apply for the openings
- An opportunity for peer interviewing and assessment of candidates
- Appropriate training for all personnel involved in the recruiting process, with special emphasis on those conducting the interviews
- An annual report as to the success rate of new hires

- Safeguards to protect the confidentiality of candidates and related materials
- A reporting system that keeps the superintendent and the board informed on a regular basis as to the status of the hiring
- An annual written analysis of those hired in terms of appropriateness of undergraduate and advanced degrees as they relate to the qualifications and experience requirements listed at the beginning of the process

It cannot be overemphasized that a single mistake made during the hiring process can have profound and damaging results for every student who passes through that teacher's classroom or that principal's building. Each time an administrator is appointed through favoritism, patronage, or political pressure, it negatively affects the district for years to come. Bad hires result in bad teaching with still more students being placed at risk.

Promoting from Within

Some districts have sufficient talent to fill all administrative positions from within and thus see no need to recruit from the outside. In adhering to this philosophy, a board must also bear in mind that employees who work for the current superintendent will most likely mirror his or her philosophy or they would not have been appointed to the position or allowed to continue to maintain their current position. That being the case, each time an inside appointment is made, the district reduces the possibility of bringing about change. Inside hiring produces clones of the current administration and its philosophy. Taken to its logical conclusion, you will eventually create a system wherein there is a comfort level that no one wishes to disturb.

A board that supports this philosophy of recruiting needs to rethink its position, for if talented administrators from outside the system are not drawn into the system from time to time, the district will most likely maintain its status quo. The district will continue on the same path, often the way to mediocrity.

Recruiting Guidelines

Because it is the superintendent who is responsible for the effectiveness of the recruiting program, regardless of who is actually in charge, there are fundamental aspects that the superintendent must guarantee:

- The board policy and administrative regulations will be accurately implemented
- Provisions of all union contracts will be adhered to
- Every candidate who applies for a position will be provided an equal opportunity to compete for and to be appointed to a position for which he or she is qualified
- All positions will be advertised in appropriate media and posted in keeping with applicable law and employee contracts
- A reasonable period of time will be provided in order that prospective candidates can learn of and apply for open positions
- All positions will be filled with the most qualified candidates after a rigorous examination of credentials and experiences
- Patronage and favoritism will play no role in the selection of candidates
- Applications for positions will be processed in an equitable manner
- The recruiting process will be transparent
- Written assessments will be created for each candidate
- All documents will be open for viewing by those who have an interest in and a right to view them under applicable law
- All evaluations of candidates will be in written form, signed by the evaluator(s)
- All interviewers will disclose any association they have or had with the candidate
- All employees who participate in the recruiting process will be educated in appropriate protocols, governing board policies, state and national mandates, and applicable local ordinances
- Any deviation from the process will be reported to the board of education

Key Chapter 4 Ideas

The superintendent alone is always responsible and accountable for recruiting.

Recruiting is the most important factor in building a successful school system.

Bad hires make for bad teachers, and bad teachers create failing schools.

Professional development will not improve the quality of staff.

Every hire must be better qualified than every other person in that department or unit.

Every board of education must develop a comprehensive recruiting policy.
The superintendent must implement safeguards to ensure an ethical re-
  cruiting system.
Fair play and a level playing field must govern all recruiting efforts.
There is no place in recruiting for favoritism or patronage.

5

Exhibit Fiscal Courage

Tax Increases

NOTHING STIRS TAXPAYERS TO ACTION faster than a proposed increase in the local school budget. Because taxpayers have no realistic opportunity to deal with education budget increases at the state or national level, the only opportunity they have to draw battle lines is locally. In their own way, the state and federal governments must be secretly delighted that citizen tax debates take place locally in that it keeps the discussion out of the state house and White House.

It is the ever-increasing tax burden created at other levels of government that makes the issue at the local level that much more critical. The more that a state government and the federal government taxes its citizens, the fewer financial resources citizens have to pay local taxes.

The tax increase at the local level is often relatively small as compared to other taxes, but it is the concept of having some control over their destiny that empowers local taxpayers. It makes little difference whether a mayor, city council, a county commission, or town meeting has approved a school budget. The mere fact that a budget will result in an increase in taxes is all it takes for the "vote no" opposition to organize. On the other side of the budget issue will be parent organizations that almost always will go to great lengths to defend increases in school budgets.

The arguments for and against a budget increase have changed little in the last fifty years. Taxpayers will condemn the increase because they claim it will drive them from the very community they helped to develop and where they supported schools for decades before the "rich newcomers showed up and ruined it for the rest of the community." The hostility between "newcomers" and "townies" is historic in large sections of the country.

Those who support a tax increase make the case that without additional funds the schools will deteriorate and the result will be diminished property values. Those who oppose the increase are considered selfish. There will be some variations of this scenario but, for the most part, it is an accurate portrayal. Battle lines are quickly drawn, and weeks and months of hostile engagements are the result. The final budget figures most often do not please either party, with each waiting for the following year and still another opportunity to engage each other. Elections often center on which politician voted for or against budget increases. Invariably there will be a change in board membership. Neighbors are pitted against one another and friendships suffer.

The fallout from local budget battles is never pleasant. This chapter describes ways to avoid creating an adversarial climate during the budget process.

Tax Revolts

On August 23, 2008, the *Wall Street Journal* published an article titled "Connecticut Faces a School Tax Revolt," which highlights that even the most affluent communities are defeating school budgets. It has reached the point where a first selectman in Connecticut proposed that his community pay students not to attend the public schools! The town would pay students a stipend to "stay away." The stipend has a value which is less than the per pupil cost of educating the students in town, thereby saving the community the difference between the stipend and the per pupil cost.

On the other hand, it is naïve of the public to believe that school systems do not require additional funding each year. Negotiated salaries account for approximately 70 percent of a district's budget, and it is most likely higher in cities and towns where budgets have been reduced (thus making salaries a still higher percentage of the total budget). Salaries in urban districts will be even higher due to the need for additional support staff. As teacher salaries rise at a higher percentage than the inflation rate, the dollars committed to salaries will increase as a percentage of the budget.

Districts across the nation are alarmed that salary demands have threatened their ability to keep pace with infrastructure needs and other fixed costs such as energy, health insurance, transportation, and maintenance. I have yet to work with a board of education that acknowledged it had sufficient funds. The flip side is that I rarely met a taxpayer audience that did not believe the schools had more than they needed. This difference in perspective is historic.

Need for Accurate Reporting of Teacher Salary Increases

One of the reasons the public has difficulty in understanding why teacher salaries continue to run ahead of inflation has to do with the way many boards of education report salary increases. Usually, the only figure reported publicly is the general increase to the salary schedule. Thus, if the general raise is in the 2–3 percent range, the public wonders why the total salary code has risen to a higher level than that percentage. The answer is simple but not often explained publicly.

What is usually not reported is the increment that approximately 50–60 percent of the teaching staff receive as a result of providing another year of service or for earning an additional degree. Increments can add another 3–4 percent to the overall cost of salaries. The remaining 40–50 percent of the staff who do not receive the increment are on the top step and receive only the general pay raise unless a special contract arrangement is made. Since approximately 50 percent of the staff will receive the general pay raise plus the increment, their total salary increase is not 2–3 percent but 5–7 percent, or more than double that which was stated publicly.

The failure to be up front with taxpayers about the true increase in teacher salaries is still another reason why taxpayers do not trust school administrators or board members. It is impossible for a superintendent or board of education to create trust with taxpayers on one hand while acting deceptively with them on the other.

On the community side, there is a similar dilemma but with a more serious twist. As community budgets suffer from increased wage demands and unmet infrastructure needs, there is a widespread belief that the schools are siphoning off a larger and inequitable share of the total funds available to the community, thus creating tension between town and gown.

Reticence on the Part of Local Officials to Address Arbitration Protocols

The public is often upset by salary increases for teachers, police, and other community employees, and almost always attaches the blame to the local board of education or the community legislative body. In reality, it is the local fiscal agency that is also to blame. They have not taken the lead to address this issue by working with state legislators, the state associations of superintendents, and the state association of boards of education to change arbitration protocols.

For decades, local officials have heard the same complaint from taxpayers about teacher and municipal salaries, and during those same years the local fiscal authority (along with the board of education and legislative body) has remained inactive in attempting to modify the rules that arbitrators use to make decisions. In certain parts of the country, all too often local authorities, including boards of education, use the arbitration issue to justify salary increases. In effect, they say "Either we grant salary increases locally during negotiations or the arbitration panel will grant them and possibly increase them."

I am not certain as to why there is this reluctance on the part of officials to tackle the arbitration issue more strongly, but it may be that they believe it is futile to attempt to change arbitration laws because state teacher organizations and other labor unions are far too powerful a lobby to confront. It is also a fact that state legislators rely upon big labor's support during elections. Local taxpayer lobbies are no match for labor unions.

Given this scenario of rising salary costs, unmet infrastructure needs, rising health costs, taxpayer revolts, and the local authority's reluctance to engage the state legislative body in an effort to change arbitration rules, local boards of education are faced with having to manage budgets that they believe threaten the quality of education. How, then, does a board of education balance growing needs with available dollars? A look at history is a good starting point.

Zero-Based Budgeting

There was a movement in the 1970s to initiate zero-based budgeting. The system, an accounting practice utilized in some businesses, was reworked by consultants for use in education. The idea behind zero-based budgeting assumes that every program and activity in a school system is evaluated every year to determine if it is to remain for another year. This was different from the traditional budgeting practice wherein educators considered only whether or not a new program could be justified and added to what already existed. Zero-based budgeting started with a clean sheet of paper with every program having to justify its existence.

The system required leaders to make difficult decisions about what remained of existing programs, what could be eliminated or reduced, and what might be added. While an excellent business idea in theory, in practice this did not happen in education. Rather, the system became more of an ideal toward which a district directed its efforts.

Nevertheless, for a number of years the movement was active and there was a high level of interest, and for good reason. The idea of examining every program in a district and determining its value to students relative to all other programs remains a sound business and educational practice. For a board of education there is much to be gained by comparing the value and cost of an elective course at the high school against the need for a remedial math teacher in an elementary school. It is enlightening to compare the cost and value of Spanish instruction beginning in grade six against the cost and need of another kindergarten teacher.

The system required a board and superintendent to discern what was essential as compared to what was desirable in its quest for excellence. It forced boards of education to get a handle on what its "big idea" was and then plan accordingly.

Derailing Zero-based Budgeting

Why then did such a promising method of budgeting fail? What derailed an apparently sensible system for making judgments about relative worth of programs? There are three possible answers. For starters, boards of education and administrators faced tough decision making. Whenever officials have to eliminate one program to advance another, they can expect significant pressure from vested interest groups. Another probable answer is that school systems did not fully believe that it was a viable alternative to the traditional method of developing budgets. It may have worked in business, but it was deemed not appropriate for school systems. The idea behind this thinking was that because programs were built up over many years, they all served a purpose and eliminating them was not an answer. A third answer was that the system was too complex for small districts with a limited number of administrators to implement it. Zero-based budgeting, if properly administered, requires a significant amount of time to review every program and to then match one against the other. For large districts the complexity of the program was not an issue given their large central office staff and the use of advanced accounting technologies. In the final analysis, neither boards nor superintendents had a serious interest in zero-based budgeting. It was profitable for consultants but not for school systems.

Boards That Lack Courage

An example is appropriate as to why boards were fearful of zero-based budgeting. Most boards find it difficult to deny a request for a new sport proposed by a booster club. An athletic booster club can be either a supporting angel or a formidable foe, much more so than advocates for academic programs. Athletic boosters in particular tend to see issues as being a win-or-lose situation. The mantra of many athletic booster organizations is "You are with us or against us."

Complicating the athletic booster issue is the fact that it is not unusual for board members responsible for decision making to also be members of the booster club and have a child interested in the sport being proposed. At the outset there is a conflict of interest.

In order to avoid being accused by taxpayers of adding a new sport at the very time budgets are being challenged, boards need to find a creative way to avoid confrontation. Requests for a new sport usually arise from a handful of very vocal parents. For example, the boosters want to introduce water polo. On the surface it appears to be a sport in which anyone who is able to swim can participate without difficulty. It is viewed as having wide student appeal. Since the district cannot afford water polo given its many other unmet needs yet does not want to offend taxpayers, the board and boosters work out a plan whereby water polo will initially be labeled a "club" sport. A volunteer will be found who will act as coach, equipment will be donated, and other expenses in the first year will be minimal with the board offering transportation. The protocols for approval will vary from community to community but will generally follow the path described.

From experience, I have learned that savvy taxpayers understand that eventually the program will become a line item in the athletic budget and will be fully funded by the taxpayer as a varsity sport. It may take several years for this to occur, but it will happen. Once that occurs, the "club" water polo program is then publicly underwritten despite the fact that some taxpayers are having difficulty meeting their monthly living expenses. These are the same citizens who would have voted against the program at the outset if the full cost of the program had been disclosed at that time. In a case such as this, a board has taken the position that what the community could not afford with one major expenditure in the first year, it will have to endure at the end of five or six years. This is also a case where the board spreads its lack of courage over five or six years rather than exhibiting strength in confronting the boosters at the outset.

Outsourcing the Management of Public Schools to the Private Sector

A second major initiative to reduce costs and improve test scores came into being during the 1980s and 1990s. There was some thinking among both theorists and practitioners that schools could be operated more economically by the private sector. Instead of school districts acting like a business, they would turn to the private sector to operate their schools. Since school districts were unable to control costs through their own efforts, there was a belief that it would be best to let private industry attack this problem. Thus was born the idea of transferring control of individual schools or entire school systems to private contractors.

Private sector contracting was similar to zero-based budgeting in that it was an effort to implement business practices but to do so using outside contractors rather than attempting reform from the inside. While there was some element of altruism in their initial efforts to operate school systems, in the final analysis these contractors were in business to make money by cutting salaries and other expenses. Therefore they had to employ systems that eventually would not be well received. In the end, private contractors would discover that they were unable to make a respectable profit and fulfill their contractual obligations to their clients. They also discovered that they could not stem the widespread opposition from teachers unions.

The idea of contracted services, supported by those ready for reform in education, met with fierce resistance from inside school systems at the outset. To begin with, there were a number of variations on the idea. Each district that contracted with a private firm put its own imprint on the contract so that there was no single model of operation even within the same district or with the same contractor.

Why Outsourcing Failed

The idea was controversial from the outset for several reasons. From the contractor side, there was a need to have complete control over personnel including the right to choose who would work in the contracted schools within the district. They wanted to handpick the staff. This implied that some staff members were not competent to work for them. Second, the contractors needed to implement their own curriculum and not be bound by what was in place. Because they were guaranteeing test results, they needed to reach their goals by their own means. They did not want to be tied to the district curriculum, which, in their minds, had proven to be ineffective. Third, they demanded control of the contracted funds. Once again, if they were guaranteeing results, they needed the flexibility to expend funds according to their needs and not those of the district. Fourth, contractors had to employ systems and working conditions that allowed them to achieve their goals and still make money. These conditions were anathema to the teachers unions, especially the conditions relating to the deployment of staff.

Union Opposition

Unfortunately, what was at stake as far as the unions were concerned was not the improvement in test scores but who was to control personnel decisions. The following were typical issues:

- The major hurdle was the idea that an outside contractor would have control over its teaching cadre and, therefore, would also have the authority to select only the most capable of the staff to work under the contractor's direction.
- Another issue was the fact that a board of education's decision to hire an outside contractor emphasized that its administrative and teaching staff was incapable of providing quality leadership and instruction.
- Additionally, the teachers unions were fearful of losing their influence in public education.
- Finally, there was what amounted to a political admission that both the district and its staff were being shunted aside in favor of private contractors.

In the end, the private contractor idea failed. Similar to zero-based budgeting, it was born of an ideal that a new initiative based on common practices in business could improve education dramatically on one hand and reduce the cost of education on the other. Had it not been so controversial with teachers unions, it may have been adopted more widely. While there were some successes, they were too negligible to warrant continuing the controversy. In the end, teachers unions were too formidable a foe for boards of education to deal with, and contracted services ended. It was still another defeat for efforts to control costs and improve education.

County School Systems

While most school systems in the nation operate at the local level with taxpayers close to the budget action, there are many states in which school systems are operated at the county level. Under such a system, budgeting is one step removed from the local populace. When this occurs, there is less of a "local feel" to budget deliberations. Nevertheless, all of the arguments for and against budget increases and teacher salaries and benefit are the same.

Those in leadership roles must still understand, whether expressed or not, that there is a pent-up anger in much of the population regarding the cost of education and that a large segment of the population is unable to fund schools at levels desired by educational leaders. The school spending spree since the 1980s was simply part of the larger national spending spree that abruptly ceased when the economy sank into crisis in early 2009.

Challenges Remain

So public education entered the twenty-first century with the same five challenges and the need to:

- Improve academic achievement for all students across the country and make all schools successful
- Fund these advancements in the face of dwindling resources
- Deal with strong taxpayer opposition to budget increases
- Contend with parent pressure for more costly programs and activities
- Convince boards of education that they must develop "big ideas" that will keep them on target and allow them to resist pressure from small special interest groups

Inept Leadership Created National Educational Crisis

It appears that those in control of public education learned little from the mistakes of the past. One serious mistake is that the public has allowed school systems to divert funds from essential academic offerings to desirable, but non-essential, activities. This scenario takes place against a background wherein too few of our talented students enter the fields of science, math, technology, and education. As a nation we have failed to create incentives for our students to major in the toughest of academic disciplines. One of the reasons magnet schools are prospering is because they are specialized schools where students are encouraged to engage in mathematics and science.

The United States produces great athletes, actors, and entrepreneurs, but it fails to produce an equivalent number of great scientists, mathematicians, and physicists. The country that invented the automobile and made it available to the masses now witnesses the decline of the industry if not its final chapter. Several other countries have educated engineers who have designed better cars at a lower price and with superior quality. Some of those same countries, along with others, have cornered the market in the design and sale of television sets, DVDs players, VCRs, and other electronic devices that are consumed in the United States.

Literally every day brings more discouraging news about U.S. manufacturing moving overseas. This shortcoming is against a backdrop where China furnishes most of our imported goods, where we continue to run up an unsustainable balance of payment deficits to other countries, and where our failure to become energy independent has resulted in the transferring of our wealth to many nations, some of which are our declared enemies.

The failure to stem the loss of manufacturing to other countries creates both a loss of jobs and a loss of business. The dramatic fallout is that there is sufficient evidence that our middle class is diminishing as a percentage of the population. Many people in our country, both native born and foreign, are impoverished.

While our Congress has failed us at the national level, our school systems have failed us at the local level. At both levels it has been the unwise use of funds, a failure to set important standards, the absence of "big ideas," the lack of vision to see what the future will demand, and the lack of courage to do the right thing. Perhaps the essential question now is not "Can we solve this crisis?" Rather, we must ask, "Is it too late?" When this question is raised, all too often the pat answer is that when the chips are down, America always rises to the challenge. When things look bleak, we always find the silver lining.

An example often used to illustrate our ability to come back from the brink is that historically we have neglected to prepare for war, but when one confronts us, we have always been victorious. Unfortunately, the current crisis is very different. In the past, we have always been victorious because we controlled the vital resources, human and material. One of those resources has been our inventive nature, and the second has been the ability to control material resources, the most vital being energy. History reminds us that Germany lost World War II in large measure because the United States erected a naval blockade, disrupted the flow of oil from the Middle East, and destroyed Germany's oil fields in Romania, fields that supplied the energy that was critical in keeping the Luftwaffe in the air at a key time in the battle for Europe.

We apparently learned little from that experience in that seventy years later America is losing the economic war because it has not secured its energy sources. The nation is also losing the intellectual war because of the low priority we assign to our educational resources, resulting in our failure to graduate men and women who can provide the intellectual and ethical leadership for our nation.

Local Boards Need to Grasp Control of Education

The primary responsibility of a board of education is the education of children. In every community, at one time or another, the taxpayer is exposed to a board's threat that if schools are not funded to the level it requested, education will suffer greatly and students will be placed at risk. A state statute is usually quoted or shown to the audience. This display of authority is for the purpose of suggesting that any reduction whatsoever in the proposed budget will cause the district to violate the statute. This, of course, amounts to nothing more than a thinly disguised scare tactic. Such statutes are designed to prohibit a board from eliminating core programs that serve all students, or that guarantee than specific services are provided, such as those for special needs students.

In order to deal effectively with funding issues, a board of education needs to be well versed in school programs. I once worked with a board budget subcommittee on which there were two financially talented business executives. Although they were often a cause of discomfort with their penetrating questions, they also brought good business thinking and practices to the table. They also left the district a process that it used long after they retired.

The primary tactic employed by the two board members, prior to the development of the final budget, was to identify three or four major program areas each year and examine every facet and line item in detail. For example, in one year they may select K-12 language arts/English, special education, and foreign language in the elementary schools. Within a three- or four-year cycle, every program offering and activity was examined. Nothing was left untouched. Since their efforts were narrowly focused each year, they were able to delve deeply into each of the programs.

Building administrators, together with the superintendent, assistant superintendent for business, and district-wide supervisors would meet with the subcommittee and together work their way through all of the details of the budget areas selected for examination. It was a form of zero-based budgeting in that every program had to be justified. There were no areas into which these two board members did not delve.

When the process began, the board members were better prepared than the administrators. They came to the sessions with their laptops, spreadsheets, and detailed data on class sizes, competing and alternative courses, budget allocation for staff, material costs, paraprofessional costs, training schedules, downstream liabilities, and historical data relative to the graduation rate of the seniors. All data were on the table, including appropriate provisions in the employee contracts that might affect any area under consideration.

Unlike most boards wherein members generally debate whether or not new programs or expansions of existing programs should be examined and a decision made as to whether or not they would be included in the budget, these particular board members were interested in all programs and why certain programs existed at all. It was a play on zero-based budgeting wherein one weighed existing programs and personnel commitments against new ones. The idea behind this effort was that existing programs and activities should be eliminated regardless of budget considerations if they served no essential purpose. As a result of their efforts, the district was able to reduce staff and programs without impinging upon the quality of instruction.

Knowing what we do about the makeup of typical boards of education, we can say it is unlikely that they would wring out of a budget anything but a modest dollar amount unless they had no other option. Furthermore, zero-based budgeting failed in the 1970s because boards of education did not have the will to eliminate programs. This is not a surprise in that many board members and board chairpersons come up through the ranks of school parent organizations and have difficulty in making the shift from being an engaged parent to that of an objective board member. Board members need to represent their constituents but must not feel bound to carry out their every wish.

Addressing the Funding Crisis

What are some possible solutions to the present funding crisis? School districts could:

- Look to the state for increased financial assistance. That is an unlikely scenario given the needs at the state level which parallel those at the local level (salaries and benefits diverting funding from infrastructure needs).
- Look to the federal government. Increased funding from Washington is an even more remote possibility given the national debt, the need to rebuild the military, the emphasis on national health care, insolvency of the Social Security trust fund, other mandated programs, and the Obama administration's pledge to reduce the tax bills for a majority of the population.
- Look to local government for relief if it comes at all. With the widespread taxpayer revolt, it is unlikely that relief will be forthcoming in the form of increased dollars; rather, it must come in the form of a better use of funds and more creative ways to increase funding outside of tax increases.

Possible Local Solutions

- We have already eliminated the possibility of making significant reductions in program offerings. The pressure from parents and other advocates is too great to eliminate anything other than minor activities. Unless there is a will to do otherwise, little will change.
- Boards could look once again to zero-based budgeting but more than likely that will be resisted by those who want still more, not less, in the way of programs.
- Attempts at year-round schools have met with resistance, primarily because the system interferes with traditional vacation periods and the long summer recess. While some cities engage in major summer programming, they are not designed to shorten the time students would be in high school. Often they are makeup programs that allow students to graduate on time. Business interests in most parts of the country do not want school beginning before Labor Day, the official end to summer. Year-round schools are not the answer to reducing costs.
- The use of vouchers and choice programs do not have sufficient mass support to reduce the cost of education. If anything, they add to the cost of education as a result of the staggering cost of bussing students across district lines. At best they are fringe efforts with little impact on the overall cost structure. Usually, when you transfer students, the per pupil money follows the students so there is no saving to the sending district.
- Another option is to design all high school programs so that students can acquire sufficient credits to graduate in three to three and a half years. Students can easily carry a heavier course load than they do now, especially if extracurricular activities are reduced.
- Still another way to shorten time in school as a financial saving is to combine high school and a community college experience into a five-year program with community colleges allowing for free and seamless movement of high school seniors into all community college course offerings.

While both the shortened high school experience and the five-year high school/community college format should be given careful consideration since they would be relatively easy to accomplish, such an effort would fly in the face of current movements in some states (including my own) to increase the number of credits required for graduation.

This movement by those in power towards requiring more total credits for a high school diploma is just another example of failed thinking in public education where more is better. Students are unsuccessful at mastering the current course requirements, so the answer proposed by our leaders is to require still more credits. It is illogical thinking turned into madness. American education and its leaders have a long history of "doing something"—almost anything—to distract from what is not working.

Again, history tells us that there is no stopping a movement that has the support of education commissioners and state legislative bodies; the movement toward increasing credits for graduation must die of its own weight, which it will inevitably do. In the meantime, much damage will be inflicted. In the introduction to this book, titled "A New Perspective," I suggested that educational leaders who are about to spend someone else's money should pretend that the money being spent is solely their own and only then decide if they would go ahead with their ill-conceived plans!

Finally, many districts engage in joint purchasing of essential materials. These efforts are usually organized through regional service centers or affiliations of local districts. These efforts have resulted in savings but do not amount to what is needed to reform the funding issue. In many other cases, districts have combined some infrastructure and maintenance programs with some benefits to the community and school district. Again, they are but a small portion of what is needed to address the funding crisis.

Education Is Behind the Times

One of the reasons education has failed to live up to the ideal of guaranteeing success for all students is that it has not kept up with the times. Elementary and secondary education in America is to world education as General Motors and Ford are to the U.S. auto industry. Union leaders in education are not unlike those in the automotive industry where the thinking is to keep jobs at the expense of product; protect the past while the future slips through its fingers; where last year's model will do; where protecting the status quo is vastly more important than the clients.

Fortunately for car buyers, they had an option and took it: they bought foreign. Unfortunately for students, most have no option but to remain with the old model and all of its defects. Only the wealthy can afford private school. Those who believed in the promise of Horace Mann are without alternatives.

Possible Funding Solutions

What, then, is the answer to increased demands for funding and demands for improved instruction and achievement while at the same time recognizing that increased funding levels will be fiercely opposed? Those who either cannot afford higher taxes or those who simply believe that public schools and town governments are hungry beasts who consume everything in their paths will be the chief opponents.

I believe that the answer lies within the responses to three essential questions that all school districts and town governments must ask. The first is "To what degree should the residential and business taxpayer be required to fund programs or activities that are outside the limits of what a reasonable man would consider to be core and/or essential subjects and services that parents, students, and educators may consider desirable?" One typical example of an answer for this question that comes to mind is "pay for play." "Pay for play" comes in a variety of options, such as paying to participate in interscholastic sports, leasing parking spaces at a high school, and underwriting expenses related to graduation. There are many more options that can be identified.

The second question is "What activities or programs should be totally eliminated from the course of studies so that taxpayers will have no responsibility to fund them directly and, additionally, they would not have to fund the expenses to pay for the administrative oversight and management of them even it they are offered at a fee?" Examples of programs relative to the second question that should not receive public funding and for which no administrative or board of education time should be used to monitor such programs could include individual or small-group music lessons by school staff, string instrument programs, freshman sports, interscholastic sports at the middle school, and other private-school-type programs. These are my examples; every district will need to determine its own priorities, which may or may not include the items listed above.

Again, these are but a small sampling of such options. Some are feasible in certain districts and others are not. For example, in urban school systems, athletics play an important role in keeping students in schools. Eliminating athletics in this situation would be a negative move in spite of the fact that only a small fraction of the student body typically can play on a team. On the other hand, what amounts to private music lessons in some districts is a cost that should be borne by parents. Each district will generate its own list.

The third question is "What major organizational restructuring is possible to further reduce overhead expenses?" This is an area that has not been fully explored. As noted earlier, there have been efforts to combine certain functions of the community and the school district. Such efforts are usually in the areas of finance and buildings and grounds. A board needs to look beyond such efforts in an effort to bring about meaningful organizational reform.

I suggest one way of looking at leadership costs. Again, it is but one example. That is, every district will need to examine the conditions that exist and seek other savings. There are thousands of what educators would agree are tiny school districts in the country. There may be an equivalent number of small school districts. Many of these districts comprise a single school and yet they have both a principal and superintendent. Other districts have two or three schools and often do not have a high school. Any experienced and successful school superintendent would agree that only a few of these districts require the services of a full-time superintendent. In my state there are several such districts that have a part-time superintendent and run perfectly. I have run such districts as a consultant and can attest to the fact that they can be led by a qualified superintendent working two or three days a week and remain highly competitive with the best districts in the state. One reason why this is not a more common practice is that some local boards believe that a district loses its identity with a part-time superintendent.

I suggest a more dramatic approach to this single issue of administrative costs. There is little reason why school superintendents in tiny and small districts in New England, as one example, could not assume the additional responsibility of operating the town government, replacing the chief administrative officer and a portion of the staff that is employed by the community. This would allow for greater integration of all services.

Most superintendents have two or more advanced degrees in education; many possess a doctorate. Their undergraduate and graduate courses invariably included work in finance, personnel management, crisis management, negotiations, community relations, human relations, and supervision and evaluation. They employ more staff than the community, have the largest budget, the most administrators, and have significantly more experience in working with the public.

There is very little in the way of management procedures that a successful superintendent would not understand or could not learn in a short period of time. With very little coursework that is specific to the management of a town, a school superintendent could easily operate both the schools and the town government. A smart superintendent would need no additional schooling and would quickly adjust to the new responsibility.

Conversely, it is entirely possible for a town manager to possess the skills to operate both the town functions and the school system. In this case, state department of education certification officials must allow for noncertified individuals, such as town managers, to operate school systems.

Benefits of Combining Roles

- There is a significant reduction in the total compensation package when you employ a single community-wide administrator rather than two, including salary, insurance, pension, and other benefits.

- When there is both a superintendent of schools and a community chief administrator, there is a persistent rivalry between the two wherein neither is totally committed to combining departments for fear of losing both control and prestige. This is understandable since "leaders" often associate size with success. But once the two positions are merged, the resistance to combining forces is greatly diminished. The ideal time to make this move is when one or both positions are vacant and new individuals need to be appointed.
- With a single human relations department, it is far easier to establish recruiting protocols that pertain to every position in the community.
- A community with all departments under the control of a single administrator will have an improved opportunity to negotiate labor contracts that are more consistent among all employee groups.

Boards of education and their executive officers have a responsibility to examine other options to save money and should do so at a time other than when they are in the midst of budget debates. It is impossible to think creatively during the pressure of a budget battle. During such times, it is natural for the board to become defensive and support the superintendent's recommendations and vice versa. It is only when the quiet of the summer arrives that a board and superintendent have the time to think creatively.

When a board and superintendent meet in strategy sessions, their first order of business should be the development of "big ideas" that set the tone, commitment, and direction for the district. Without this, the board and superintendent simply vacillate from one budget crisis to another. They end up pitting taxpayers who are not using the schools against taxpayer parents. They yield to the noise of vested interest groups and ignore the needs of students who have an interest in world languages and not in crew. Their lack of commitment to propel the system to excellence sets them on a course to mediocrity. It is their responsibility to make schools successful.

Boards of education need to think big, act aggressively, be forceful in setting the direction of the district, and use their power and influence to satisfy student needs, not their personal needs or those of vested interests. Alternatively, school superintendents need to implement with enthusiasm and energy those goals established by the board, keeping in mind that more is not better.

Key Chapter 5 Ideas

The local budget process invariably creates conflict.
Arguments for and against any increases have not changed.

The "townies versus newcomers" issue is historic.

Taxpayers believe that teacher salaries have siphoned funds from infrastructure.

Paying the least competent the same as the most competent is a problem.

Both zero-based budgeting and private contractors failed to stem increases in costs.

With little learned from history, educators in the twenty-first century address the same historic challenges.

Boards must examine creative ways to manage with diminishing resources.

Superintendents should be able to operate both schools and local government in small towns in locales where this is practicable.

6

Provide Objective Oversight and Assessment of Superintendent of Schools

Assessing Superintendent Performance

IF THE SUPERINTENDENT IS NOT powering a school system forward in such a manner that students are learning at ever-increasing levels of achievement, it follows that the entire system is enveloped in an educational stalemate. It is for this reason that a board of education's assessment of its superintendent is vital to the success of a school system, for if the leader performs at journeyman levels, then that is the level at which the staff will perform.

While assessments of school administrators have a long history, it is a history often marred with a lack of effectiveness. There are a number of reasons for the lack of positive experience with assessments:

- To begin with, many boards of education simply fail to evaluate their superintendents. The reasons vary from one district to another but in the final analysis these boards simply have no interest in formal assessments. They will make judgments about performance, renewal, or termination of its superintendent based on often undisclosed reasons or reasons that are unrelated to performance.
- Second, when boards do conduct assessments, they often fail to use a valid yardstick against which to judge their superintendent. The primary reason for this is that when a board does not articulate its "big ideas" it also fails to provide the superintendent with the proper direction or incentive to promote the district. It is simply business as usual, another day at the office with no major initiative to be assessed.

- Third, assessments are often based on issues that have little impact on student learning. They fail to use, as a primary objective, the improvement in student learning. One reason this occurs is because boards have a tendency to utilize "off the shelf" assessment tools developed by state or national associations of boards of education or those developed by organizations representing superintendents. By themselves, such tools miss the target in that they include many areas of responsibility that, while important, do not sufficiently measure student achievement and have little to do with making schools successful.
- Fourth, there are boards with members whose sole aim is to harass or terminate the superintendent and, therefore, assessment tools are devised solely for the purpose of exposing what these members believe to be shortcomings and reasons to terminate the superintendent.

Assessing Instructional Leadership

It is against this backdrop of limited success that modern assessments take place. Unlike the practices of the last several decades, some boards of education have now recognized that it is imperative that superintendents be assessed on goals that are directly related to improving student learning. All other goals are secondary to those that guarantee student success. The competition our students face from those of other advanced nations is so fierce that American schools must subjugate almost all programs to those that advance the intellectual ability of their students. Our industrial might has been compromised by our failure to graduate students who are capable of reigniting our inventiveness and creativity, the undergirding of our former strengths.

What we have lost as a nation will not be recaptured with a potpourri of electives, outstanding athletic programs, and highly desirable music, art, or physical education activities. While all of them are vital to a well-rounded education, it is a fact that there is not sufficient time in the typical school day to have both a challenging academic program and a wide variety of other student programs and activities. Many of these programs, if not all, must be offered outside of the school day with funding derived from sources other than taxes.

The Olympics make for great viewing and a temporary pride in our country and its athletics, but they contribute literally nothing toward the survival of the nation. The United States is long past the time when it could afford the luxury of ignoring intellectual development in all students. There must be an end to the watering down of the curriculum, and the institutional attitude that expects some students will not succeed. In successful schools, no student will fail.

We are a nation that is having difficulty in maintaining itself as a world power in the twenty-first century. In many ways it has lost its focus, and the only route back is through its schools. Boards of education must be at the vanguard of this renewal. School superintendents are the front-line soldiers in this struggle. For this reason, boards must assess the work of school superintendents based on whether they have created an environment that not only encourages student success but promotes it. Without outstanding success at the local level, there can be no national agenda for improvement.

Quality assessments are not only more important today than in the past but are more complex because of the collaborative model of leadership. This is a model most superintendents employ; one that diffuses responsibility for the running of the district among many administrators. Because of this diffusion, it is a challenge in itself to determine who has the responsibility for the lack of success in our schools. When test scores are poorer than expected, who is to blame? Is it the leader of the district or the leader of the school? Is it the superintendent or the lead curriculum specialist? What responsibility does a board of education have to shoulder such a failure?

In order for any assessment to be effective in an environment in which authority is dispersed, a governing board must first define the essential role its superintendent will play. It should not depend upon the "off the shelf" tools mentioned earlier that describe the several areas in which the superintendent will be assessed. A superintendent must first be judged on the degree to which the four major goals of the board of education have been effectively implemented. If those goals have been met, the system prospers. If they are not met, the district treads water.

Four Assessment Goals

It is worth reviewing how the four goals of a board of education serve as tools to assess the work of the superintendent.

- If a board accepts the premise that the most important of it four goals is the creation of "big ideas," then the primary role of the superintendent is the implementation of those ideas. What is clear is that if a board of education is not a "big idea" entity and views itself as little more than a bureaucratic body that rubber-stamps the administration's agenda, then the district is not in a position to break out of its generic brand label. If, on the other hand, a board is a risk-taking body and emboldens the district with its big ideas, then the superintendent plays the major role in bringing the goal of the big idea to fruition. When the big idea is directed at student achievement, then the district is well on its way to developing successful schools.

- If the second most important function of the board is the development of a powerful and equitable hiring policy, then another expectation the board has of the superintendent is that the policy is fully and accurately implemented, that safeguards are in place, and that periodic written reports as to its effectiveness are provided to the board. A board of education and superintendent would have to be in denial not to accept the premise that the strength and quality of any school system is a direct result of the quality of those it employs. If time and effort are not expended at the beginning of the recruiting process to employ only those who can move a system forward, then human resources will be expended later in a futile attempt to remediate the problem after significant damage to students has occurred. A board of education and superintendent either build strength into the system with recruiting or it will forever be behind the curve. To be truly effective, the recruiting process cannot be tinged with favoritism or politics.

- The third goal of the board, fiscal responsibility, presents a challenge for the superintendent in that once community financial resources have been allocated, they must now be distributed internally to enhance student learning. This means that priorities must be established and programs compared one to the other to determine what combination of academic programs and student activities will provide the best guarantee that this school district and its individual schools will be successful. This goal will be challenged when some parents and other vested organizations, such as booster clubs, have their own ideas as to where to expend these funds. And, if that were not a sufficient challenge for a superintendent, there are outside agencies or enterprises that want to influence school offerings or make grants for the right to have athletic complexes named after their companies. Superintendents are constantly under pressure to allow outside commercial interests to make contributions in payment for entry into the schools. To those who would question the author's inclusion of "fiscal responsibility" as one of the primary goals of both the board and superintendent, one only has to examine the pressure the average superintendent is under just to manage a budget. This goal is the most difficult for a superintendent to accomplish in that he or she is under pressure to improve student learning while being confronted with diminishing resources on one hand and challenges to the school budget on the other. It is not an enviable position to be in.

- The fourth goal, the assessment of the superintendent, is the subject of this chapter. It identifies and explains the four major areas that a board of education must utilize in assessing the work of its superintendent.

Three of the four goals noted in this chapter should be utilized directly by the board in its assessment of the superintendent. The fourth goal, the oversight and assessment of the superintendent, also provides an area of assessment for a board since the superintendent can be judged on the degree to which he or she has developed and maintained data relating to all goals and that the board can utilize to make an assessment. Chapter 7 illustrates nine additional areas of assessment that a board may consider using to expand upon the basic four goals listed in this chapter.

Key Chapter 6 Ideas

The work of all superintendents must be accurately assessed by boards of education.

Assessment of superintendents is one of the four primary responsibilities of a board.

Many boards do not assess the work of their superintendents for various reasons.

Other boards do not perform quality assessments.

Most boards fail to assess a superintendent's performance on how he or she directly improved student achievement.

7

Additional Areas Available to Assess the Work of the Superintendent of Schools

Changing Role of the Superintendent

I MAKE THE CASE IN CHAPTER 6 THAT every board has four major areas of assessment, both for itself and the superintendent, but there are additional areas that a board can consider using to assist it in making judgments about its superintendent. Before considering these other possible areas of assessment, it helps to examine the changing role of the superintendent and how it affects what a board should look for when it assesses the work of the superintendent.

For the last two decades, superintendents, in their quest to improve test scores, have relied heavily upon curriculum specialists. These specialists, many of whom have never taught in a regular classroom or managed a school, have been entrusted with a critical aspect of the district, that of nurturing the core academic program. Utilizing this design, many superintendents have relegated themselves to being overseers of the process rather than providing hands-on academic leadership.

Although superintendents work closely with curriculum specialists in their employ, they also leave the expertise to them. Rather than the superintendents being the academic leaders of a system and employing others to handle the management details, they have reversed roles and assigned the responsibility of the academic program to subordinates. In my opinion, this is one of the major reasons schools have not been successful in improving student success rates. It is one of the reasons schools are not successful. Rarely will you witness a superintendent engaged in a public dispute with a member of the public over the reading materials in the third grade; more than likely you will witness a dispute over the use of artificial turf on the football field, or whether or not the district can afford a marching band. When you add to this equation the fact that most superintendents now practice the "collaborative" leadership model and employ "site-based management," we have provided still other avenues of retreat from responsibility for superintendents by allowing them to further delegate their responsibilities to building principals. On the surface this is a way to share responsibility. It is also a way to cast blame elsewhere.

Additional Areas of Assessment to Be Considered

Once a board of education is committed to the four primary goals, it has other optional areas of responsibility it should consider assessing. What it selects will depend upon the nuances of the district and the level of success of the superintendent. If a superintendent has performed in a manner that the board finds effective and satisfactory, it can ignore some or all of the following. If, on the other hand, there is reason to believe that the superintendent's efforts have not contributed significantly to student success, a board may want to look to one or more of the following areas for assessment purposes.

Academic Initiative

The superintendent should be among the most academically talented of the staff. If anyone on the staff should possess a quality undergraduate and graduate education, it should be the superintendent. A board should exert caution when reviewing a superintendent candidate's undergraduate degree in particular and look for those who have strong academic records. Little emphasis should be placed on graduate degrees in education since many college of education professors rarely assign a grade below an A minus, and a C is almost unheard of. Professors well understand that education courses are the cash cows at most universities, and they are not about to rock the boat. Because of the lack of classical academic preparation on the part of most superintendent candidates, boards of education must be careful not to place too much emphasis on style at the expense of substance.

Time Away from District When School Is in Session

Most teacher and administrator contracts have clauses that prohibit staff members from taking personal leave before or after a holiday or leaving the district early on such days. Yet it is not uncommon for superintendents and other central office administrators to take such leave, usually justifying it on the basis of their heavy workload and the inability to leave the district when school is in session. When examining this rationale, boards need to keep in mind that the total compensation package of a superintendent, including golden handcuffs and golden handshakes, takes into account the workload and responsibility of the position. Superintendents need to set examples for their employees.

If board members want a realistic example of what constitutes a heavy workload or the inability to have a minute of quiet time at any time during the school day, with long hours in a pressure environment, simply examine the role of a building principal, especially an elementary school principal. It is worth remembering the old saw: "What is good for the goose is good for the gander."

General Attendance Record

This category is to be considered as a basis for assessment in that it is impossible for a superintendent to effectively manage a district long distance. When I was a search consultant, I cautioned a number of boards on the problems inherent in hiring specific superintendent candidates who spent an inordinate amount of time with superintendent organizations at both the state and national level and who attended far too many out-of-district and out-of-state conferences, seminars, and other meetings or conventions, or spent time as members of visiting accreditation committees or regional accreditation organizations. These absences are self-satisfying and look impressive on a resume, but do little to improve the quality of schooling for students back home. Little of what takes place at such functions will directly benefit students at home.

A board needs to employ superintendents who develop a sensible schedule for being out of district. A board should require a quarterly report on out-of-district commitments. Participation in training sessions must be relevant to improving student performance. It is vital that superintendents select training opportunities that are of value to the district and not primarily of benefit to the superintendent. Every district needs a leader who is well versed in new strategies and programs, especially if a board expects the superintendent to be the academic leader.

Quality and Frequency of Evaluations on Administrative Staff with Emphasis on Improvement of Instruction

It has been mentioned that the most important job of the superintendent is that of hiring. Hand in hand with that responsibility is the careful evaluation of those who have been hired. In small districts, the evaluation of building level administrators is the responsibility of the superintendent. In larger districts, the superintendent will usually evaluate assistants and deputy superintendents. The issue remains the same; the superintendent is responsible whether he or she directly supervises principals or delegates this job to assistants and deputies.

A board is remiss if it fails to validate that such evaluations have been completed, are directed at the improvement of instruction, are accurate assessments, set the stage for school success, and have been discussed with the employee. A board needs assurance that appropriate assistance has been provided to the employee and that the evaluations have been completed and have been made part of the official file.

Too often principals are evaluated on items that have little relevance to student learning but that are given equal weight on evaluation forms. A superintendent is as good as the quality of his or her subordinates, and failure to regularly and frequently assess their performance with regard to improving instruction will inevitably lead to a diminished school system.

Time Spent with Teaching and Administrative Staff in Training Sessions

It is important to teachers and administrators that the superintendent be present at some of their training sessions. Employees correctly make the assumption that a superintendent is incapable of understanding the complexities of teaching and learning, or course content, without walking in their shoes. Most superintendents have not been in an elementary or secondary school teaching capacity for many years, some for decades, and do not have direct, contemporary experience in the challenges facing the classroom teacher. Teaching as an adjunct at a university does not compensate for this shortcoming. One way to earn the respect of teachers and have a realistic sense of contemporary teaching is to be part of staff training sessions. In larger districts, such attendance may be limited to training sessions for administrators. A board must be cognizant of the degree to which its leader is present at training sessions and must not accept as an excuse that he or she is too busy to participate. Being present for a few minutes to demonstrate "attendance" does not meet the goal of participation. Leaders need to set positive examples.

Time Spent in School Buildings and Specifically in Classrooms

"Walk the Talk" is the mantra for effective CEOs in American industry, but it has become more of an ideal than a practice in American education. From experience gained during my role as a search consultant, I know that a newly minted or appointed superintendent will launch full speed into visiting schools and classrooms. Usually, it is a promise made during the hiring phase. In small districts, superintendents make it a point to cover as many classrooms as possible, while in large districts they attempt to visit special programs or important sites in the district. This may last for a year or two, and then a steady decline in visitations will occur.

The rationale employed is that there is little time in the day to make visitations on a regular basis. This reasoning is often valid, but more often than not it is the failure to restructure work schedules so that instruction is the first priority. It goes back to the fundamental question as to the role of the superintendent: caretaker and manager or visionary and instructional leader?

Provision for Periodic Feedback Sessions with Teachers and Administrators

As a search consultant, it was an eye-opening experience to conduct focus sessions with constituent groups to receive feedback important to the search process. The board of education that hired me approved the focus sessions as a way to learn more about the district and its employees in order to select a superintendent who could address any current or emerging issues. Search consultants quickly learn what is positive and what is troubling employees. I cannot think of a single search wherein employees did not ask why the board and superintendent did not hold focus sessions of their own on a semiannual or annual basis to listen to their concerns.

There is much to be learned through this process. Two recurring themes almost always surfaced at these sessions. First, in literally every district in which the author conducted searches, the paraprofessionals would mention that they received little or no respect from a fair number of teachers and occasionally from the principal. The second theme is that in small districts in particular, with a limited staff, superintendents did not take the time to learn the names of secretaries, clerks, and paraprofessionals. Both themes are personnel issues, and all administrators and teachers should understand that employees want to be acknowledged by name. Superintendents need to develop the common touch when dealing with subordinates in particular.

Responsiveness to Ideas from Teachers and Administrators

Focus sessions serve a purpose as noted above, but they are not the appropriate forum to hear from staff on ways to improve instruction. A board must take an interest in the formal strategies a superintendent implements to elicit ideas from the professional staff that benefit students and the school in general. Those on the front line in a district are often light-years ahead of experts and consultants when it comes to employing new instructional strategies.

Much can be learned from them. Highly paid consultants are not the answer to a district's troubles.

Sessions with Students

Search consultants almost always meet with high school students, and occasionally with middle school students. As in sessions with staff, one learns a great deal from students. They will tell you that it is more important that they know you care before they care what you know. I recall two occasions when students devastated two school boards with their revelations. It was apparent that neither board was aware of the issues. As it happened, the students were in two high-performing districts.

First student feedback

In this instance, the student was president of the junior class and ranked number one. This was a large and extremely wealthy district. At a public forum during the search, in front of a very large and involved audience of parents, citizens, community officials, employees, the board of education, and others, he presented an impassioned accusation and an emotional plea to the board. The accusation was that the board and administration had ignored those students who performed at or below expected academic standards and whose negative behavior was partially the result of having been ignored. These students came to school with no hope that they would be in classes that had any meaning for them. He claimed that whatever disruption these students caused was the fault of the administration for not addressing their needs. Too many resources were allocated to students like himself who already had more than he felt was needed. His plea to the board of education was to make things right by providing a relevant school experience for these students. The board hired a new superintendent whose primary mission was "to make things right."

Second student feedback

In the second instance, I was meeting with a group of high school students representing all four grades. There were no other adults present. The students made it clear that in this high-performing high school the only thing teachers were concerned about were test results of the academically talented. On the other hand, the staff and administration ignored what these high performing students referred to as "The Invisible People," those "other" students who were not part of the intellectual elite, and who "flew under the radar screen." For them, high school was a daily trial with few course offerings that met their needs, and a lack of attention from an unsympathetic staff and administration. There was literally dismay and shock on the part of the board when the consultant reported this. They had no idea that such a condition could exist in their system. The board hired a building principal as its superintendent, an educator who had experience with alternative programs offered within the context of a regular comprehensive high school.

Conclusion

Both of these student stories argue for listening to our clients, including the students. The nine areas noted above, in addition to the four major areas outlined in chapter 6 that are appropriate for both boards and superintendents, comprise the thirteen categories that can be utilized in whole or in part by a board in assessing the work of its superintendent. There may be others that are deemed important in any given district, but if one or more of the nine optional areas of assessment I recommend are selected by the board, depending upon the prior performance of its superintendent, and are met at the highest levels of achievement, one must believe that a district will be rewarded with successful schools.

Key Chapter 7 Ideas

The assessment of the superintendent must be one of the four major goals of a board.

Many superintendents are either not assessed or inappropriately assessed.

It is imperative that a quality assessment of the superintendent takes place.

Collaborative leadership makes it difficult to assign blame.

I identify four basic areas of assessment and nine optional ones.

Student feedback is critical to any board when it assesses its superintendent.

8

Strategy Number 2: The Superintendent of Schools Providing Academic Leadership

Leadership Styles

THIS CHAPTER ADDRESSES WHAT I believe to be an area that requires a considerable upgrade by superintendents in their district's quest for educational excellence and successful schools. The topic was introduced in the first chapter, where I made the case that boards of education typically do not hold superintendents accountable in the appropriate areas.

Typically, boards utilize the same standard checklist-type assessment tools in rating superintendents as they use for themselves. It isn't that these standard checklists omit items related to student achievement; it is that they include far too many other items, many of which are mundane and routine. They have a way of distracting both the board and the superintendent from the most critical items.

Many of the tasks listed in standardized assessment tools are associated with lower level administrative activity. They should play only a minor role in assessing a superintendent. To give more than a passing look at these tasks is to invite average performance and leadership. Superintendents should be evaluated on far more important and pertinent issues. This chapter will explore what those issues are.

"Old Style" Leadership

One of the reasons so many superintendents are assessed on irrelevant matters has to do with the prominent leadership style that is employed today. It is considerably different from the "old" style that was associated with the "strong leader" type. The "old style" superintendent leadership model was "top down." Ironically, its development was the creation of a "bottom up" philosophy. To become superintendent one had to start at the bottom of the pyramid and work his or her way up the many steps of the career ladder, most often and preferably in the same district.

It was not unusual for superintendents to have a physical education and coaching background. They were thought of as being "tough" and knew how to deal with discipline in the schools, one of the main criteria to becoming a principal and then superintendent. It was not unusual as late as the 1960s to pay selected teachers a stipend to help with discipline because they were thought of as being tough disciplinarians.

The old style of leadership was not unlike that of the military where you proved yourself on the field of battle. It was a style that tended to keep order in the ranks. The old style was criticized. Many critics, especially teachers, union leaders, and university researchers, sought new and more effective leadership styles. Nevertheless, the old style served education well at a time when challenges were easily identified and problems minimized and easily resolved. It was a time of little oversight by the governing body, limited parent involvement, and a society with an insensitive and uncaring attitude regarding service, diversity, and equity.

Comparative test scores were interesting but not essential to the conduct of school business. Parents played a minimal role in the schooling of their children. Accountability was not important. Parents generally did not want to have much to do with the schools. The truth is that principals and teachers frightened most parents; consequently the attitude of parents became one of "leave it to the educators."

In the 1960s and 1970s, education witnessed the beginning of a shift in parent attitude, which the general public shared. With the launching of *Sputnik* in 1957, pressure mounted from the business sector to graduate more qualified students at both the high school and college and university levels. Also, Western Europe had fully recovered from the devastating effects of World War II and was competing with the United States for global financial dominance and market share.

The G.I. Bill had provided millions of young men and women with undergraduate degrees and/or training in the trades. Veterans wanted a better life for their children and viewed education as the route to get there. State legislatures began to adopt standards for education and the federal government began to impose sanctions if schools did not implement specific policies dealing with diversity and equality. In the meantime, business had been developing new leadership models for itself. Eventually some were adapted for use in education.

"New" Models of Leadership

One of the business models which caught the interest of educators was Japanese "Quality Circles." This became the leadership buzzword of the 1980s. It was a style that worked for business but eventually had only limited success in education in spite of repeated efforts to incorporate it. In the end, the time required to implement and sustain "Quality Circles" was a major hurdle that could not be overcome in education because of the time constraints, particularly for building level administrators whose daily demands left little time for Quality Circle conversations with co-workers.

Education then made other efforts to "flatten" the organizational structure without the complexity of Quality Circles as a way to draw others into the decision making process. The goal was to reduce the staff at central office and move day-to-day decision making into the field. It suffered from the fact that while decision making was moved to the building level, resources were not. The central office remained the arbiter of all things financial.

Strategic planning then became the next major effort to refocus the organization. Initially, it became the popular answer to distributing responsibility because it was a school- and community-wide attempt at involvement and supported the flat organizational pattern. While it plays an important role in many communities, it has lost some of its appeal. Only remnants of this process remain. Quality strategic planning requires far too much in the way of oversight and monitoring. Only the largest of districts with a major central office staff could keep the system up to date and working properly. Like so many other initiatives in education, it had a quiet and unnoticed passing.

In spite of changes to leadership style over many decades, schools do not improve at a rate needed to halt the decline in student achievement. In reality, no "new" leadership style had proven to be more effective that the old top-down, "strong leader" approach. In the meantime, our culture had changed and employees wanted a larger role in decision making. A new model of leadership was needed in education. Unlike business, in which major decisions can literally be made overnight and new products and services implemented at "Mach speed," educational decisions are made at "snail speed." Because of the slow pace of implementation, change was often by osmosis. A new leadership style was needed.

Current Leadership Model

This new leadership model is one of collaboration, a method of leadership that recognizes the contributions of others, shares decision making, thinks of schools as "profit centers," and creates committees as a way to distribute responsibility. It has been successful to the degree that less controversy is generated in a school system as a result of the elimination of top-down management, which staff often views as a dictatorial style.

Unlike top-down leadership or one-person decision making, collaboration spreads the risks inherent to leadership. With a collaborative style, tasks usually are accomplished, however long they may take. In spite of many positive attributes, the collaboration model suffers from the fact that it is cumbersome, uses time of professionals inefficiently, and affords all central office personnel the opportunity to share blame as well as share leadership. It is a style that affords the superintendent the opportunity to hold others responsible for failures in literally every area of school life. It affords leaders the opportunity to delegate not only their responsibilities, but their accountability as well.

All things considered, collaboration is probably no more effective, and perhaps even less effective, than the old top-down management style. This is especially true when we consider the inability of the public school system to bring every student up to the most minimal of proficiency standards and in spite of the vast financial resources that have been committed to the system. One cannot help but pause and consider if still another leadership model is needed since the current one has not been successful in attaining needed academic proficiency for all students.

How Collaboration Has Failed Students

The following is a good example of how collaborative leadership has failed, especially in small and medium-sized school districts. Under the old model, superintendents were in charge of education, and they made decisions thought to be the best for accomplishing any given goal. Since at least the 1990s, however, superintendents have relied upon curriculum specialists to develop, implement, and monitor the academic program.

Utilizing this design, superintendents have relegated themselves to the role of overseers in the instructional process rather than providing hands-on academic leadership. While they may work closely with their curriculum specialists, they also leave the expertise to them. Instead of superintendents being the charismatic, powerful, engaging academic leaders of a system and employing others to handle management details, they have reversed roles. Superintendents have become the managers and their subordinates have become academic leaders. Is it any wonder, then, why public education has not lived up to its promises to educate every child to the fullest?

Boards of education need to carefully consider the leadership style of superintendents they are about to employ. This is especially important in districts that perform poorly. The purpose of this recommendation is to determine the degree to which candidates have a working knowledge of curriculum, and to determine the amount of time they have spent in previous assignments at the grassroots level with teaching staff.

In the case of superintendents already employed, a board needs to examine the amount of time superintendents spend on management details that can readily be delegated, thus freeing critical time for a superintendent to be in schools and in classrooms. It is impossible to implement change at the building level if one does not witness firsthand and on a continuing basis what transpires in classrooms.

When superintendents rely solely upon others to observe and report on classroom activity, he or she runs the risk of receiving "filtered" information. The only true quality control a superintendent has relative to teacher effectiveness is to be present in schools and classrooms on a regular basis! This is especially true when supervisors doing the reporting are members of Unit B of a teachers association as opposed to being in a stand-alone administrative bargaining unit.

One of the most damaging decisions that superintendents and boards of education make in reducing budgets because of taxpayer resistance has been to reduce key members of the central office staff. It is, or course, the easiest place to cut and has the greatest visibility, but it results in the superintendent being responsible for far too many areas of responsibility. It is one of the reasons superintendents do not spend sufficient time with the teaching staff and in classrooms.

Students Still Fail

Most experienced superintendents want to believe that they provide outstanding educational leadership to the staff and district. It is also natural to be defensive if anyone challenges this idea. Nevertheless, the fact is that with a fair number of exceptions, mostly in wealthy districts and magnet or charter schools, public education has not lived up to its ideal of assuring success for all students.

I realize that multiple arguments will be presented to the contrary and many success stories cited. These stories cannot be denied. Yet with half of all students in a wealthy state such as my own not meeting minimum proficiency standards, how can the public, who pays the bill, believe that schools are successful? The story worsens when you realize that "proficiency" is the lowest level of achievement.

Academic Leadership

This brings the reader back to the basic premise: the lack of success in our schools is people-related, not curriculum- or program-related. What education really faces is the need to implement a leadership style that is primarily academic and not managerial. I am of the opinion that until we train an entire generation of superintendents who will grasp control of the academic program, we will continue to witness lack of success for all students. The dilemma is that millions of students, especially those in urban and rural America, cannot wait a generation; they need help now.

As a working superintendent, one sees but one version of leadership; his or her own. Each has an opinion as to the leadership style of colleagues but because they do not work for them, what they know about them is what they learn second or third hand. Thus, what you know about leadership is what you personally practice. In the final analysis, whether or not your personal style is successful remains for others to judge.

As a general educational consultant one witnesses as many versions of leadership as one has clients. How accurate your impression is of the style will depend upon how long you are engaged with the client. What you soon realize is that there is significant variation in the academic leadership provided by superintendents. As a search consultant (as opposed to a general consultant), too, you are exposed to many styles; literally as many as you have candidates! The further along candidates proceed in the process, the more accurate is your impression. You soon realize that other men and women are powering their districts to higher levels of achievement primarily because they have an academic orientation and feel comfortable challenging ideas generated from their own staff. As a percentage of all superintendents, the number of such men and women is small.

An Example of Academic Leadership

What exactly is the "academic leadership" that is expected of a superintendent? What is expected of academic leaders? Why is it important that a district have such leaders? First, it implies a challenging exchange with educators in the district who propose a course of studies, with those who teach the courses, and with those who ultimately decide what is an essential program versus a desirable program. For example, it is not sufficient to have a discussion with the high school principal as to when Algebra II is taught or what the sequence of courses will be in science, or whether band will be scheduled during the activity period or lunch period, or when academic classes are in session. That hardly qualifies as academic leadership. Far more important is a discussion as to:

- Why is the course in the program of studies to begin with?
- Who will teach the course?
- What are the teacher's credentials?
- What documentation is there regarding this teacher's rigor in other courses?
- To whom will it be taught?
- What are the prerequisites and why?
- What safeguards are in place to ensure equal access?
- What are the standards for awarding a specific grade in a course?
- How do you control the quality of multiple sections of the same course?
- What evidence is there that grade inflation is not embedded into the culture of the school?
- Who has the authority to alter the courses of study and why are they being altered?
- What impact will this course offering have on other courses?
- How will the success of the course be measured?

These are but a few of the many questions that must be asked. They provide an idea about the level of required participation by the superintendent and the depth of inquiry that is required.

Second, academic leadership means having the courage to establish priorities. The following are examples of the questions leaders must ask themselves in their quest for excellence. There is an endless list of possible questions.

- What is the justification for a new varsity sport when elementary school students need additional reading assistance?
- Why would limited funds be used for travel and memberships when a chemistry class has more students than lab tables?
- Why would a district expend funds for a convocation speaker when computer labs are in need of new equipment?
- Why would the district schedule a summer retreat off-site for administrators when library funds have been reduced?

Leadership is a way of thinking and acting. Without the willingness to leave convention behind and employ the simple words "no" and "why" to desirable but not essential programs, there is no leadership!

A Thought or Two About Academic Leadership

In my experience, academic leadership means that the leader grasps the moment to propel a district forward in keeping with the vision and 'big ideas' of a board of education; a time to demonstrate to the staff that educators represent a cause, a mission, and a movement that demands excellence in classroom performance. The leader must inspire a staff to new levels of excellence, be visible, be supportive, be questioning, be provocative, be inspiring, and, above all, be exemplary in behavior, speech, action, and ethics. Leadership means what it says: to lead, to show the way, to open vistas, to promote, to inspire others to follow, and to succeed. It is a quest, a passion, and a way to reach the ultimate goal of improved achievement for all students.

"Strong man" leadership may now be considered the old model of leadership, but it never lacked in inspiration and zeal. It moved staff from inertia to action. It dared to go where the faint of heart would not tread. It bred an entire generation of risk takers. With its passing, education has suffered because the system has neutralized our leaders. We have made them compromisers, negotiators, and collaborators. We have weakened them, and undermined them with our goal of satisfying all constituents. Now our students pay the price.

Finally, academic leadership is about students, not adults. Academic leaders accept suggestions from parents, but do not make them the decision makers. Leaders respect some of what a vested interest group may desire, but do not place value on their noise or threats. Leaders make it abundantly clear to the staff, the board, and the community that they are in charge of academics and they will make decisions that address basic student needs and not the desires of adults.

My experience, both as a superintendent and consultant, is that teachers and administrators want strong academic leadership from a superintendent as long as it is in a culture that respects employees and that has established the parameters of fair play and equity. Outstanding superintendents create a culture in which there are no surprises, in which all employees understand the consequences of their actions. The saying "What goes around comes around" may be prophetic in that perhaps the time has arrived to develop a generation of leaders who practice the "old model."

Loving Children Is Not Sufficient

As a search consultant, I met hundreds of superintendent candidates from every type of school system in the nation: large, small, rich, poor, urban, suburban, and rural. I met practicing superintendents, those who aspired to the position, and those who had lost their positions. I met new ones and experienced ones. Some loved their jobs, others dreaded their jobs, and there were those who were indifferent to their jobs. They ranged from brilliant men and women to those who had no right to be superintendents. Many were then currently successful, while others were not. What was striking about all of them was that during their interviews they all stated, in one way or another, or in response to a question, that they were "committed" to children. Often, they said they loved children or that children were the "first priority." It is a given in education that if you are a teacher or administrator, you must love children. There should be no reason to doubt that they did.

But that response always raised a more provocative question for me: Is "loving children" the same as educating children to their potential? Does being "committed" to children imply that you operate a district with successful schools? Do the words get translated into action? Does it mean that every child in your care is achieving at his or her maximum? Does it imply that all elements of outstanding leadership are in place? In the final analysis, the proof is in the pudding.

Key Chapter 8 Ideas

Academic leadership is a vital characteristic of the successful superintendent.

Many superintendents have delegated academic leadership to subordinates.

There is a question as to whether academic leadership and collaborative style are compatible.

There is much to be said for the "strong" leadership style.

Curriculum specialists have become academic leaders and superintendents have become managers.

Collaborative leadership has produced compromisers and negotiators.

Successful schools need a strong superintendent who is the acknowledged academic leader.

9

Strategy Number 3: Instructional Power at the Building Level

Unappreciated Leaders

THE ONE ELEMENT OF INSTRUCTION THAT all superintendents will agree upon is the essential role that building principals play in the improvement of instruction. In my many roles during a long career, I spent significant time working with principals. In my experience principals, along with the superintendent, played the key roles in bringing academic excellence to the teaching process. However, unlike superintendents who govern from a distance, building principals are the frontline advocates in the drive toward academic excellence. They are the energy source needed to bring about improvement. In addition to the responsibility for the instruction program, principals juggle multiple tasks, often under the most trying of circumstances.

Elementary school principals in particular work in a high-pressure environment. It is not a case wherein elementary principals work harder than secondary principals; it is just that parents are a constant presence in elementary schools. Some are aggressive to the point of being unreasonable, and others are often uncontrollable. Most elementary principals are without an assistant, which means they have little or no opportunity for quiet moments in which to reflect on the educational process.

High school principals, though they have assistants and are able to find relief during the day, are burdened with an evening and night schedule that challenges that of the superintendent. Their compensation does not take into consideration the time they spend in school.

Principals at all grade levels are the power behind instructional improvement at the building level. They are responsible for translating mandates from the board and superintendent into a plan of action. Under the management style now in vogue, they are also held responsible for the failure of academic initiatives. In addition to this major responsibility, they are held accountable for literally all other aspects of managing a building, including disciplinary matters.

Talented principals at all grade levels are unique human beings in that they need to know when to push, when to hug, when to fight, and when to withdraw. Of all the administrative positions in education, this is the one from which we should choose our heroes. As a former superintendent for twenty-five years, I have profound admiration for talented principals and have taken a public stand that of all educators, they are the ones least appreciated and least rewarded for their efforts.

When Talent Really Counts

Parents, central office staff, and even board of education members are quick to identify outstanding teachers and heap praise on them, all the while forgetting that it is the principal who has created the climate in which teachers are able to perform their duties and exhibit their craft. Just as there are no outstanding school systems without an outstanding board of education, neither are there outstanding teachers without outstanding building principals.

Principals need the unqualified support of the superintendent and central office staff. All too often they are the educators held responsible for students not meeting proficiency levels on state tests when the real culprits are insufficient support from central office, marginally qualified teachers assigned to their schools, inadequate support staff, demands on their time for administrative meetings, and far too many staff members to evaluate. Few educators have the talent, the perseverance, the interpersonal skills, and the will to be outstanding principals. Is it any wonder that principals make such great superintendents?

How Instructional Improvement Works

If principals are the power behind instructional improvement, what then are the conditions that must be in place for this to occur? Given the complexities of attempting to raise academic achievement for all students, it is a given that this will not occur without a plan of action. What does the principal have to do and what does a superintendent have to contribute to bring success to the process? An example will serve to help understand the roles to be played.

It is best to start at the beginning where the reader must assume that a board of education's "big idea" to be implemented over the next three years is that in grades kindergarten through grade three the only subjects to be taught are language arts, mathematics, and science. Furthermore, the equivalent of only one period a day will be available and shared with all other subjects that will henceforth be considered activities. It means that social studies, music, art, and physical education will be offered in short modules on a rotating basis. Social studies as a full subject is to be deferred until grade four.

The board's reasoning is that many students do not read at grade level, academics generally have suffered in the district, there has been but limited progress to improve achievement, the day cannot be extended because of financial constraints, and it is totally unacceptable to have students leave the third grade unprepared for the many academic challenges ahead. The board arrived at this conclusion after considerable discussion among its members, input from appropriate staff, central office personnel, and other members of the administrative and teaching staff. There is a belief on the part of most educators that the nation produces few scientists and mathematicians because students have limited exposure to these subjects in the early years. Students are not encouraged to appreciate these subjects in part because of the lack of talented teachers to instruct them. The board believed that the only option to address this challenge was to implement the "big idea" noted above.

The superintendent's role in this process, after he or she provides expert advice and counsel to the board, is to pave the way for full implementation. Both the board and superintendent were prepared for serious opposition from both the staff and the parents. The changes are dramatic and far reaching. It is at this point that the superintendent demonstrates academic leadership by taking the initiative to explain the reasoning behind the board's position, defending the initiative against those opposed to it, and providing unqualified support to the principal as he or she begins the complex task of implementation.

If a superintendent is not articulate and persuasive, not committed and enthusiastic, convincing the constituents will be a much greater task. On the other hand, the superintendency is not the position to hold if one is not able to address and convince audiences of the need for change in order to improve instruction for all students. A successful superintendent must be an articulate public speaker.

Principals As Leaders

It was mentioned earlier that change can mean alterations in employee schedules, and possible displacement and termination of personnel. The "big idea" of teaching only language arts, mathematics, and science in the early grades is dramatic in its consequences, and calls for dramatic shifts in personnel. There is now a limited need for teachers of social studies, art, music, and physical education. On the other hand, there is a greater need for teachers of language arts, mathematics, and science. These modifications need principal and superintendent leadership.

In this illustration, it is at the principal's level that academic leadership occurs. Any educator who has had experience working in elementary schools understands that there is a special relationship between principal and staff members. The elementary school resembles a family environment in which trust is the most important ingredient. If any one person is able and qualified to gain the support of the teaching staff, it is the principal. If a principal does not believe in the educational mission, it will fail. A superintendent who fails to recognize the loyalty that an elementary principal commands from staff and parents does so at his or her own risk.

Outstanding principals have a following among teachers and parents that a superintendent and board can never develop. The fact is that the vast majority of superintendents and boards have no group following! It is difficult to imagine parents with placards marching in support of a superintendent.

Without the total support of a principal the "big idea" has little chance to survive. If the "big idea" described above is to succeed, it requires the total commitment of three parties: the board, the superintendent, and the principal.

How a Principal Becomes an Academic Leader

There are many facets to the role of principal as academic leader, but there are five activities that define his or her level of academic leadership. They are as follows.

Participation with Staff in Training Sessions That Are Relevant to Improved Student Achievement

It was stated earlier that a superintendent must be part of appropriate teacher training activities. There are few better ways for a superintendent to demonstrate to staff that he or she is the academic leader of the system. The same philosophy holds true for the principal. There are two aspects of this issue. First, training sessions must be carefully planned such that they address the primary goal of insuring that instruction is outstanding and that teachers receive the appropriate training. Guest speakers and sales representatives do not meet the test of providing effective training skills. The best instruction for staff will most likely come from their peers in the district. Second, the presence of the principal emphasizes the importance of the session. It also highlights the fact that the person in charge of this institution is both knowledgeable about instruction and also has a clear understanding of the challenges that teachers face.

Spend Quality Time in Classrooms with Students and Teachers

If a principal wants a quick read on who the outstanding teachers are in a building, he or she can simply ask members of the staff for an invitation into their classrooms. Invariably, it will be the outstanding teachers who will be first to extend an invitation. They want the principal to observe their work and they want the principal to interact with their students. A principal needs to establish an environment in which even insecure teachers look forward to having the principal in their classrooms. When the principal is part of the classroom scene on a regular basis, he/she creates a positive relationship with the teachers and students.

Prepare Quality Assessment of Teacher Performance

No educational institution can meet the challenges of students unless the level of teaching is of the highest caliber. There is no effective way to measure instructional quality other than a skilled observer being in classrooms on a continuing basis throughout the school year. On one hand, the principal needs to establish a positive environment by being present in classrooms as noted in the previous section but, on the other hand, there comes a point when judgments need to be made as to the quality of teaching.

It is not sufficient to simply assign the principal the key role in the assessment of teacher performance. There is an obligation on the part of the school system to provide training in assessment and to then make certain that time is allotted so that the principal can complete this important task. In this regard, superintendents need to be mindful of the impact of having principals leave their buildings for meetings and other peripheral work. It is unfair to teachers if the assessor is ill prepared.

Create a System That Encourages Teachers to Share Ideas

The primary thrust of this book is that school systems have historically placed far too much emphasis on materials and outside experts to solve the issue of student failures when the answer lies with extant personnel. Every school system and every school building has its fair share of outstanding teachers who have in one way or another mastered the art of teaching without having had to resort to still another workbook, textbook, program, or piece of technology. Their success comes from their ability to understand the give and take in the teaching and learning cycle as well as how students are motivated and learn.

Superintendents must find a formal way to access this wealth of talent at the district level and principals must do likewise at the building level. My experience is that once a system is put into place to utilize local talent to teach other teachers, staff members will come forth in large numbers to be part of the new cadre of instructors for training sessions. Teachers, in their role of trainers, take great pride in acceptance by their peers. Conversely, teachers on the receiving end of this instruction take pride in a profession that recognizes one of their own as outstanding.

Commit the School to the Philosophy That No Child Will Be Left Behind

Long before the federal No Child Left Behind legislation was enacted, quality school systems had embraced the concept that every child had the right to a quality educational experience. It was not always that way in public schools. It took special-education legislation decades ago to sensitize the American public and our school leaders to the fact that there were students who were not being fairly treated. Had it not been for federal legislation, special-needs students would still be seeking assistance. Public schools have come a long way since then to remedy this shortcoming. Nevertheless, there still remain large pockets of underserved students. They are mostly, but not exclusively, minorities.

One of the often invisible of the underserved is the rural poor. Without political clout, they have no influence at either the national or state level to politick for additional aid. But wherever they are and whoever they are, there is a need to make certain that they are brought into the educational mainstream. While a board of education may mandate that there be no "invisible" students in the school system, and assuming the superintendent puts into place administrative regulations to address this need, it will always remain the principal who is the guardian of this guarantee.

No one person in the school will have a better understanding of the student body and the subgroups within it that require special attention and care than the principal. Remedial services must be readily available and there must be constant monitoring of student progress. There must be an attitude that all children can learn if provided the professional services of teachers in a school that embodies the American dream that every student is equally special.

The plea that the high school junior made about the administration failing students who were not part of the intellectual elite and the comments of the high school students who spoke about the plight of "the invisible students" rings as true today as the day they spoke. It remains for the superintendent and principals to guarantee that schools are successful in reaching all students including those who are "invisible" or operating under the radar.

Key Chapter 9 Ideas

Principals are the educational heroes of the moment.

Principals are the power behind instructional improvement.

Outstanding teachers need outstanding principals.

"Big ideas" cannot survive without the support of principals.

Teachers respond to principals, tolerate central office personnel.

No educator understands the nuances of the student body as well as the principal.

Relative to superintendent compensation, principals are grossly underpaid.

10

Strategy Number 4: Establish Ethical Hiring Standards

The Key to a School District's Success

THE VITAL ROLE THAT A BOARD OF education plays in a district's professional recruitment system was the subject of chapter 4. This chapter highlights the equally vital role that the superintendent of schools plays relative to the recruiting process. For both parties, recruiting is the first step in building a powerful school system.

My second book, *Recruiting Strategies for Public Schools*, was published by Rowman & Littlefield in partnership with the American Association of School Administrators. Some of the following ideas and materials are excerpts from that book and relate directly to the role of the superintendent in implementing a board of education policy on recruiting. These materials were edited or reorganized to be consistent with other materials in this book.

Upon arrival in a school system, the superintendent needs to take charge of the hiring process. The recruiting process is the single most effective way for a superintendent to set the tone and direction for a school system, particularly a system seeking improvement and change. Unfortunately, most superintendents do not remain in their positions for a sufficient period of time to dramatically affect the quality of the staff. Those who do remain often fail to understand the importance of setting ethical standards for recruiting.

In the same sense that reading is the most important subject taught and the basis for all other learning, recruiting is the most important function a superintendent performs and is the most critical step in building a powerful school system. A superintendent must surround himself or herself with the best talent available at all levels of the organization. This talent should bring a variety of values and ideas for improving education.

Knowledgeable superintendents who remain in their positions for any length of time understand that the recruiting cycle begins with a comprehensive policy statement and administrative regulations. Superintendents need to urge and encourage a board of education to develop such a policy. It is an essential ingredient of an effective hiring program. Without a vision for recruiting, a district will migrate from one crisis to another. Hiring is job number one.

In addition to providing guidelines for the staff as it engages its recruiting cycle, a policy has the strength of law for the staff and provides substantial protection to a superintendent and the school system as they honor every candidate and as they work tirelessly to maintain a level playing field. A superintendent who is unwilling or unable to guarantee that every candidate has equal access to an open or new position is failing students and the district. For that reason alone, one can justify a strong board policy on recruiting.

Superintendent Guarantees

The most objective way to protect the rights of job candidates is for a superintendent to vigorously support "Three Basic Guarantees." They are moral and ethical mandates that a superintendent must shoulder, regardless of who is overseeing the recruiting process.

The First Basic Guarantee

A recruiting protocol must be based on an underlying belief that all new hires into the school system must and will be appropriately inducted. This implies a formal, ongoing, and appropriate orientation program. It also assumes that only a small percentage of new hires will meet all of a district's professional criteria at the time of hiring. Although a district never achieves perfection in a hiring program, perfection must remain its goal. Perfection is achieved only after a recruiter has contracted with the most outstanding teachers and administrators available at the time and has implemented a formal entry program to induct them into the school system.

An induction program also processes experienced, but often professionally immature, educators. A district makes a serious misjudgment if it assumes that years of experience are equivalent to professional maturity. It is important to be mindful that a twenty-year veteran may have had the same experiences twenty times over! We have all heard of teachers who work from the same lesson plans year after year regardless of what the current curriculum may be. A recruiting policy must make it readily apparent to whomever is making the final hiring decision that all potential new employees must be judged in part on their willingness to participate in an induction program, regardless of their prior experience level.

The Second Basic Guarantee

The superintendent must be an educator who champions contract language with the local teacher and administrator representative groups. There are two provisions that are especially important. The contract must have a highly competitive salary schedule for all employees but, in particular, for entry-level teachers and administrators. So often, the most experienced teachers are on the negotiating team and they tend to "take care of those at the top."

Occasionally, a district will get lucky and employ someone who needs a job at that particular moment; or someone whose spouse is transferred and where the move requires a candidate to take the first position offered; or someone just plain desperate for work. She or he will take the compensation offered. However, it would be professional suicide for a district to depend upon luck to staff its schools.

A superintendent must also fight for a contract provision that allows him or her to hire at any step on either the teacher and administrator salary schedule without first receiving the permission of the teacher or administrator associations. This flexibility provides a great opportunity to hire the most outstanding candidates. Hand in hand with this contract condition, the superintendent must have the ability to convince the governing board that she or he must not be restricted as to where on the salary grid a new teacher or administrator may be placed. To be competitive in the marketplace, a superintendent must be able to use placement on the salary grid as a recruiting tool.

A superintendent cannot use as an excuse the fact that board members or a governing board's attorney negotiates the contract and that he or she had no role in its development. Superintendents are paid to be aggressive in promoting what is best for their school systems. A superintendent must be able to hire teachers and administrators without the prior approval of the governing board.

The Third Basic Guarantee

The hiring process must have an impenetrable firewall that separates it from the patronage system. This is easier said than done, but a superintendent must have the courage to confront the patronage issue. When patronage is mentioned, one might logically assume that it describes the political pressure that is applied to the human relations personnel, the superintendent, and governing board members when friends, relatives, and political cronies of powerful politicians apply for employment. This pressure comes from outside the school system. Indeed, it is a powerful force, sometimes overwhelming. It is the most common type of pressure and is often visible to others.

There is also a second form of patronage that emanates from the inside and is not often visible from the outside, but that must also be confronted. While there are no official data available, it is a well-known fact that a high percentage of administrators are married to other educators. It logically follows that spouses and other family members of superintendents will be employed in other districts and in the same districts. In these instances some percentage of superintendents will come perilously close to penetrating the patronage firewall in the manner in which they process applications of relatives of colleagues. In some instances they will, in fact, penetrate it.

Superintendents need to keep flawless, potentially public records of the interviewing process, particularly the written assessments of candidates that were completed at all stages of the process. They also need to be explicit in their directions to employees who were engaged in the hiring process that there will be no exceptions to the prevailing written protocols.

Justifying All Hirings

A superintendent must be able to justify to an objective third party, such as local radio, television, and newspaper reporters, that the hiring of friends, relatives, and others who may be related to other superintendents or other influential educators is within the parameters of the recruiting guidelines and/or official policy. Any exceptions can lead to his or her undoing.

The media have proven to be unrelenting in pursuing alleged wrongdoing, especially when it involves high-level public officials. Such public exposure could seriously compromise school administrators—who, the public wants to believe, maintain the highest ethical standards. Even though a school administrator may believe he has won a media battle, he may well have lost it in the minds of the general public. Worse still, the resulting discredit has a way of clinging to a school system and public officials forever.

Yielding to patronage is an ugly event unbecoming all public officials, especially superintendents who are entrusted with furthering the well-being of children. It is inappropriate for school superintendents to bemoan outside pressure that may be applied to them in the recruiting process while using the system for their personal advantage or that of colleagues. Either form of patronage is debilitating to a school system because it sends a clear message that the playing field is not level.

Large urban systems that have a powerful-mayor form of government are most susceptible to the patronage game because of the enormous influence the political structure has on school funding. To ignore this pressure takes a superintendent of considerable strength and character.

Superintendents employed in rural areas and small suburbs are also subject to outside pressures. Often, one or two families "run the town" or have considerable influence over town politics. They are as skillful at applying pressure as big city politicians! Superintendents in these districts face pressures not unlike those of their urban counterparts. Newer, emerging pluralistic suburbs are less likely to feel these same intense pressures since many of those in political positions are new to the community and have little long-term influence.

The "Three Basic Guarantees" may not be written into the recruiting protocols, but they are the silent conscience of a quality recruiting program. The superintendent must safeguard them at all times. Leadership is measured in large part by how one vigorously defends what is morally and ethically correct.

During my fifteen years as a search consultant, I witnessed numerous instances when a board practiced favoritism. There are two types of appointments made to an open position that are disheartening to a qualified candidate who is not appointed to the position. The first is to see an insider appointed and to later learn, by way of professional networking and gossip, that the insider was the superintendent's or governing board's choice from the beginning. The interviewing process was merely used as a formality or "legal cover." The second type of appointment that shakes the confidence of candidates is that of the outside "favorite."

Insider Favorites

First, let us a look at the "insider" situation. The "insider" label is employed in this section to identify anyone who is employed in a district, but not necessarily in the same building or unit where the vacancy exists. An insider appointment usually occurs when the district has an employee who, although he may not be the best candidate, has considerable support from high-ranking administrators, particularly the superintendent or governing board members.

There are several reasons why an insider may be appointed to a position ahead of a more qualified candidate from outside the district, as noted below:

- A new superintendent may use an "insider" appointment as a way to build instant popularity with others in the district by allowing an employee to become an administrator without really earning the position.

- It may be used to pacify insiders who objected to the former superintendent's philosophy wherein all positions were widely advertised and which frequently resulted in positions being filled by more qualified candidates from outside the district.
- Some governing board members may believe that a particular insider "deserves" the new position; for example, someone who was especially helpful to a governing board member's children or who is popular with the student body.
- Someone may have been around for many years and thus has "earned" the position based on her long tenure.
- An insider may be promoted to a new position primarily to remove him or her from a currently held position.
- An insider may be appointed because the superintendent is an adjunct professor in a university leadership program and promotes those in that university program who also happen to work for him or her.
- An insider may be appointed because he or she is part of an internal leadership training program, or promoted to demonstrate that the program works.

There are other reasons insider appointments are made, but whatever the reason for promoting an insider, it will always be the wrong reason if the process is tainted. Appointing an insider based on any form of bias is no better than yielding to political or patronage pressure. A governing board that tolerates such a system is shirking its oversight responsibilities. A superintendent who promotes insider appointments to gain professional capital threatens the integrity of the entire recruiting process.

Full Search Required

It is difficult to build power into a system if there is not a full-scale search that reaches out to as many potential candidates as possible. A leader has no idea as to the effectiveness of an internal leadership program unless insiders in the program go head to head with those from the outside and with others on the inside who believe they are locked out of the process. No matter how qualified a particular insider may be, there must be a competitive comparison with others. If, however, the search is already tainted by virtue of the insider having the support of the internal staff, then no search should be conducted and a direct appointment made forthwith.

A superintendent's role in a search is similar to that of a private search consultant in that the process for selection must be transparent. Anything less is unacceptable. I have advised governing boards that interviewed me for their search consultant not to conduct a search if there is a strong tendency to hire an insider.

When a board has a favorite, the search amounts to a sham and brings discredit to the district and humiliation to the candidates who apply from the outside. It also diminishes the reputation of the consultant. Applying for and competing for a position is a stressful event; a candidate does not need the humiliation of competing for a job that is already spoken for.

Assume, for the sake of argument, that the insider has no apparent advantage in that no one encouraged her or him to apply and there is no particular reason why he or she should receive the appointment. In other words, there appears to be a level playing field. The process is as it should be. The recruiter still needs to take three precautions.

- First, all inside candidates should be informed that they will receive no advantage simply because they are insiders. The only exception may be a contractual one with the local teacher or administrative associations wherein a governing board agreed with the associations to interview all insiders regardless of qualifications.
- Second, anyone who is involved in the recruiting process in any way must be informed that the playing field must remain level. For example, it may happen that the insider may ask a clerk or friend in the personnel department how many applicants there are for the position. Innocently, the clerk or friend may reveal this information and more, such as the names of the other applicants. This is a violation of the ground rules since no other candidate has access to the information.
- Third, the interviewers in the process must be informed that an insider is to be given no advantage. Even though an insider may have more information about the district than an outsider, this is no reason to believe that it makes the insider more qualified.

An insider may have more local data, but this does not make him or her any better qualified for the job in question. So often this is used as a way to justify an inside appointment.

Outside Favorite

The second type of appointment that threatens the integrity of the recruiting system and shakes the confidence of all candidates is that of the outside favorite. How does this work? It resembles the insider activity in that a high-ranking individual in the district "encourages" an individual employed in another district to apply for an opening.

The candidate applies believing that she is the favored candidate. In fact, when someone applies through invitation, it is reasonable for her to believe she is a front runner or a finalist for the position. The higher the rank of the person soliciting the candidate, the more confident the candidate is in believing that the position is his or hers. In some cases, there may be no advertising for the position as a way to limit the number of applications.

The interesting point about "inviting" an outsider to apply is that an insider who applies without invitation believes that the process will allow him to compete when, in fact, the position is essentially promised to an outsider. It reverses the discrimination that was explained in the insider job placement case.

It is through recruiting that a district has the most effective opportunity to propel a district upward to a status that places it among the best-performing school systems in the nation. It follows that if the recruiting system is flawed in any way, the opportunity to improve a school system begins to slip away. Putting brakes on a system sliding downhill is far more difficult than pushing it uphill to excellence. Once a district acquires a reputation for not operating its recruiting system in an open manner, it diminishes its ability to attract the best candidates.

Key Chapter 10 Ideas

Recruiting begins with a comprehensive board policy and regulations.
All superintendents need to take responsibility for the recruitment process.
The policy must allow the superintendent to hire staff at any step and scale.
Superintendents must vigorously defend the rights of all candidates.
Firewalls must be established to prevent bias and prejudice from infecting hiring.
Internal promotions must be weighed against outside competition.
Insiders must not be appointed solely because they are participants in an internal leadership program and are used as evidence that the program works.

11

Strategy Number 5:
Appropriate Staffing Levels

Educators Where You Need Them

WHILE THE BOARD OF EDUCATION IS, in my opinion, the most important of the seven strategies in a school system's climb toward high achievement, it also determines both the existence of and the quality of other strategies. For example, if a board fails to develop a strong and equitable recruiting policy with a full administrative implementation, then the second most important strategy for high achievement is missing.

Whenever a board of education fails to fully employ its complete authority—does not use its power to determine the shape of a district's initiatives by implementing all of the seven strategies—then the district is at best stuck in neutral. Without the full complement of seven strategies, all working simultaneously, a district is unable to reach its goal of high achievement for all students. Progress is never linear and often exhibits erratic shifts, but the momentum of the seven strategies tends to bring the inevitable swings within manageable limits.

One of the strategies that a board of education has full control over is strategy number five, which addresses staffing levels, the subject of this chapter. Earlier, I presented an example of a board of education exhibiting dynamic academic leadership by establishing a priority wherein the need for additional teachers in language arts, mathematics, and science took precedence over any other program. That example addressed a specific academic shortcoming that needed to be resolved. Social studies, art, music, and physical education were provided with considerably less teaching time in the day for students in grades

K-3 so that language arts, mathematics, and science could be allotted more class time.

It is this type of decision making that defines academic leadership for a board of education. It alone has the responsibility to guarantee that both teaching and support staff assignments are at levels where students will be appropriately served. A board's political courage will be tested as it sets new priorities that require the superintendent to redeploy human resources to meet challenges.

The Board Controls Staffing Levels

While the board has complete control over staffing levels and assignments, this is the one strategy that also requires the full support of the board, the superintendent, and the principal. Although input from the teaching staff is essential to decision making, it must not be the determining factor in establishing a district's priorities. Even outstanding teachers may have personal agendas that do not coincide with those of the district. The decision making responsibility regarding staff levels belongs to the board of education and, in this instance, to the superintendent and principal. This point is best made if we consider an example.

Assume for a moment that the board of education, after examining test data in detail and after conferring with members of the staff as to the inferences one could reasonably draw from the data, concludes that students at the Alfred Street School are performing well below expectations in basic reading skills, the subject from which all other academic successes flow. This information was known to prior boards of education in the city and to both past and present administrations. However, insufficient work was undertaken to address the problem. The current board took office with a mandate from the public in general and Alfred Street School parents in particular to bring all schools to a point well above state proficiency levels.

As part of its analysis, the current board examined the student-teacher ratios in grades K-3 and found them to be in the average range of twenty-four to twenty-six, not unreasonable in terms of state averages but unacceptable in terms of meeting the needs of students at the Alfred Street School, a school enrolling some of the most educationally deprived students in the city.

For years, the answer to this dilemma was that there was inadequate funding to support smaller class sizes. However, each year there were increases in the budget for many other activities, but no additional funds were set aside specifically to reduce class sizes in grades K-3. Over the years adequate materials were made available along with expert consultants. Neither the plethora of materials nor the consultants were successful in stemming the failures in reading for grades K-3.

Value of Small Class Sizes

Almost to a person, elementary school teachers and administrators will agree that small class sizes are necessary if every child is to have the full benefit of outstanding teachers. Providing small class sizes to marginal or incompetent teachers would make little or no difference in outcome. For that reason, the recruiting program must employ only the best educators.

Ostensibly, a class of fifteen to eighteen students in the care of an outstanding teacher will make the difference between success and failure for many students who come to school with serious language deficiencies. There are probably thousands of classrooms in urban districts across the nation in which there are new students who speak no English whatsoever. Yet they are expected to learn at the same pace as students with some English proficiency.

Compounding the problem is the fact that in this era of inclusive classrooms, the continuum of teacher responsibilities is expanded considerably, making it impossible to give attention to all who need it when class sizes are in the twenty-four to twenty-six range.

Given the unfavorable test data, the board concluded that the lack of student achievement was directly tied to the large average class size. The most reasonable response to the problem is to create smaller class sizes in grades K-3. The next step is to identify and divert funds from programs and activities that have a lower priority and direct them to employing or transferring teachers to grades K-3. This decision demands the full support of the superintendent, the principal, and the teachers.

Reshuffling of Priorities Is Essential

In the earlier example, the solution to resolving a deficiency in reading was to defer the teaching of social studies and reduce the time in art and music and transfer teachers of those subjects to subjects with a higher priority, in that case reading. The solution in this second example is basically to leave other staffing unchanged and reorder priorities in nonteaching areas in order to stem the flow of failures among K-3 students. Among the victims may be football, instrumental music, guidance, administration, summer workshops, and administrative and board retreats, travel, and seminars. Basically, everything must be placed on the table that is not a fixed cost.

When a board makes a potentially controversial decision such as suggested above, it will undoubtedly create turmoil among some constituents. There is a moment in time when educational leaders must take a stand for children. On the other hand, the stand must have the positive outcome of dramatically raising community awareness that improved student achievement is the primary goal of the school district.

Principals Make Three Guarantees

In the course of making its courageous decision to redeploy staff, the board of education must make certain that the principal who implements the moves addresses three other concerns:

- First, the principal needs to guarantee parents that all teachers assigned to grades K-3 are capable of teaching reading to all students. It makes little sense to assign teachers to this problem area if they lack the qualifications to address the needs of students. This in itself may require redeployment of staff with the inevitable personnel conflicts that will occur.
- Second, the principal and staff must make certain that, rather than depend upon average test scores to determine success in any one grade, data must be disaggregated in order to ensure that each subgroup is examined separately, that each individual child with a deficiency is identified, and that additional resources be assigned or reassigned as the data dictates. This is what really is meant by "No child left behind."
- Third, the principal needs to examine the experience of the teachers involved to ensure that their background is suited to teaching K-3. A teacher may have the necessary certification and experience, but not be qualified if personal characteristics or demeanor to teach in a given grade are left wanting.

Key Chapter 11 Ideas

Appropriate staff levels is one major key to success.
Creativity in course design must be exhibited.
A board's courage will be tested when systemic priorities are reshuffled.
Listen to staff members, but understand that they may have personal agendas.
Board members must fight and defend small class sizes in grades K-3.
Teacher assignments must be based solely on qualifications.
Students in need must quickly receive remedial assistance.

12

Strategy Number 6: Tenure Track or Performance Track

Teachers Unions Have Gained the Upper Hand

IN SEVERAL OF THE PREVIOUS CHAPTERS reference has been made to teachers in a generic sense. Many of those references were less than complimentary to the teaching profession as a whole. It is convenient for any critic of education to make the case that teachers, as a unionized group, have been party to the current situation in our schools along with board of education members and school superintendents. There is sufficient blame to go around. This situation is primarily due to the fact that most teachers, concerned with salary and generous benefits, march in lockstep with the teachers unions.

Few teachers at the local or state level take issue with the leadership even if individually they disagree with union positions. Individual teachers have too much at stake to risk offending the union power structure. While outstanding teachers would certainly be open to a system of higher compensation based on performance, they are fully aware of the union position.

From the very outset of teacher negotiations in the 1950s and 1960s, unions fought successful legal battles to take control of working conditions in school systems. It turned out that teachers unions, even at the local level, were far more experienced and prepared in the art of negotiations than were boards of education. They had learned from industrial unions, such as the AFL/CIO, that power to control an organization lay, not in higher salaries, but in controlling work rules! Their national and state associations provided them with considerable mentoring. Consequently, boards throughout the nation were simply outmaneuvered. This resulted in their relinquishing valuable work rules while initially winning on salary issues.

Little did boards of education realize that the party who controlled work rules literally controlled the professional staff. Eventually, arbitrators addressed salary issues to the benefit of the teachers. This was a lose-lose effort for boards of education. It took them several decades to realize how badly they had blundered in these negotiations. They have more recently attempted, with little success, to "buy back" that which they had given away. Arbitrators are reluctant to take from unions that which they won through negotiations.

Today, teachers unions continue to demonstrate great ability in negotiating contract language that provides them with significant power in shaping the working conditions for teachers on one hand, and restricting the authority of the boards of education and school administrators on the other.

Management Adheres to Contract Language

If there is relative peace in a school district, it is because management is adhering to contract language that invariably benefits the union. There is hardly an assignment or transfer of a teacher that is not subject to contract language that requires union approval. Efforts on the part of administrators to change duty rosters, class assignments, length of teacher lunch periods, number of preparations, posting of positions, and meeting schedules are mostly controlled by contract language. Contract language practically controls every administrative effort to deal with employees. Unions have a dominant presence in local education governance and have tied the hands of management. They are not about to relinquish this power. If the situation was reversed, neither would the administration or board.

National teachers unions play the same powerful role in education that the United Auto Workers (UAW) plays in the automotive industry. It is worth noting that the American automotive industry has been strangled to the point of going out of existence. While management is partly at fault for not building cars of better quality and mileage, the demise of the industry is more likely attributed to unfavorable work rules that tied the hands of employers, and the generous health and retirement benefits given to workers. The National Education Association and the American Federation of Teachers have a similar hold on the educational enterprise.

Balance of Power

The education enterprise must acknowledge that it is literally impossible without national or state legislation to alter the balance of power between unions and boards of education. Given the size and strength of the union lobby, legislative remedy at any level is, at best, remote. No union will willingly give up its position of strength regarding work rules.

Arbitrators are reluctant to support board efforts to make simple changes in contract language, let alone dramatic changes. Politicians at the state and national level are dependent upon union support in their reelection and fundraising efforts, and are unwilling to make statutory changes that negatively affect unions. The status quo remains relative to work rules in education.

What remains as a somewhat viable possibility is a change in the way districts compensate teachers, which would encourage more outstanding individuals to enter education. Hundreds of efforts have been made nationwide to compensate teachers in a manner that is different from current practice. There have been some minor successes pertaining to merit pay. Nevertheless, teachers unions on the whole have resisted any major change in the way districts compensate teachers unless such change benefits all teachers regardless of their skill level. The single salary system has long been ingrained into the educational enterprise, and any effort by boards to dislodge it or alter it is a major issue for the union. The answer, therefore, does not lie in its elimination; rather, it begs for an option alongside it.

Teacher Salaries and Benefits Create Public Anger

The public, in defeating school budgets, is almost always concerned with the total education budget. But what infuriates taxpayers are teacher salaries and benefits combined with the work-free summer. There is also concern that all teachers are paid the same salary based on years of service and degrees regardless of their ability, which is linked to the student scores on standardized tests, National Assessment scores, SAT/ACT average scores, and advanced placement results.

As expected, parents, students, management, and taxpayers are well aware of the fact that there are marginal teachers receiving the same salary as outstanding teachers. They do not need administrators to tell them who these teachers are.

This system of payment, the single salary schedule, simply means that there is but one way to compensate teachers regardless of the quality of their performance or difficulty of their assignments. For example, an English teacher who almost always can be counted on to take papers home to correct, someone who spends considerable time in preparing for class, is paid the same salary as a physical education teacher who has limited class preparations and little or no work to take home. They both are assigned to teach the same number of periods.

Assume for a moment that if all other things were equal, the poorest-performing social studies teacher is paid the same salary as the best physics teacher. Added to this concern is the fact that the least able teachers, as a result of tenure statutes combined with timid administrators and weak boards of education, essentially have lifetime employment. It is small wonder that the public has not revolted against this system, which in no way resembles what is done in private industry with professional level employees.

Alternative Method of Compensation

It is my contention that the quality of instruction would improve and education would attract and retain outstanding teachers if the union leadership allowed for a reasonable modification of the workforce compensation issue. Such a modification would also have the by-product of diminishing the hostility between taxpayers and teachers. In the long run, both parties would benefit, but it is for a board of education to address this issue and consider it a "big idea" worthy of its time and effort.

The essential question is, why is there a need for an alternative system of compensation? As mentioned in the opening paragraph of this chapter, teachers as a group have been referenced throughout this book and not always in the most favorable light. Yet it is clear that there are tens of thousands of outstanding teachers whose compensation is no better than that of the marginally competent among them. Some will argue that, as a percentage of the total teacher population, the number of poor performers is small. However, for the student who is assigned to a marginal teacher, the percentage argument put forth by the union is moot!

I am more inclined to look at the teacher population as a distinct universe, much like a universe of police officers, lawyers, stockbrokers, doctors, or school superintendents. Each universe falls on a bell curve and, while the argument may be made that a bell curve for teachers can be skewed such that it is weighed to the competent side, there is no data to support that supposition.

If we can accept the bell curve theory of distribution, then approximately 68 percent of the teacher population falls within one standard deviation from the mean. This percentage represents our journeymen teachers. They are competent, hardworking, dedicated, and generally meet district expectations. Basically, they are paid a fair wage for the work they perform. There are few stars among them.

As you move from the one standard deviation towards each end of the bell curve you will have teachers working below the norm and others working above the norm. At the extreme ends you have a population that is outstanding and a population that is marginal. This raises two issues:

- How does a school district justify compensating the poor performers the same as the outstanding performers? The fact is that school systems cannot justify this arrangement but nevertheless continue to employ it. One has trouble identifying any other professional occupation in which the worst performer is paid the same as the best performer. It defies logic that the public has allowed this system of compensation to become institutionalized.
- The second question is fairness to students. Which courses are taught by the outstanding teachers and which courses are taught by the marginal teachers and why?

An essential question was raised earlier: Why is there a need for an alternative system of compensation? The answer is that it is unfair to the taxpayer to pay the best teachers the same compensation as the worst teachers receive. This does not occur in any other profession. There is an equally important second essential question. Which teachers do you want your children assigned to, the best or the worst? The answer being obvious, a district must then negotiate a system that compensates the thousands of outstanding teachers fairly. On the other hand, it must not continue to automatically increase compensation either for the journeymen teachers or the marginal teachers.

Tenure Is Vital to Teachers and Should Be
Not Challenged but Supplemented

If a board and union have the will to develop an alternative system of compensation, it must first address the matter of tenure. This is of paramount concern to the union and its membership. As difficult as it is for a school system to work with tenure statutes, they should not support efforts to eliminate tenure. It remains a key component in teacher employment and is a benefit that teachers unions will never relinquish.

Rather than deal with the matter of tenure head on, negotiators for both parties should explore whether there is an option that both parties could accept, and that preserves tenure while still providing for an alternative way to attract and compensate outstanding teachers. It is a challenge of immense proportions but not without realistic possibilities.

Tenure Track or Performance Track

This chapter explains one specific idea for a board of education to consider in its efforts to improve student learning. It may have been tried in some isolated districts that I am not aware of. I first proposed it in October 1984 to the Connecticut Governor's Commission on Equity and Excellence in Education. At the time, the commission was looking to dramatically increase all teacher salaries and was not interested in a new method of compensation. The idea presented, however, is but one notion that could work and it addresses many of the concerns that a board and a union may have relative to the tenure issue.

My proposal is for an optional system of compensation that I refer to as "Tenure Track or Performance Track" System, or TT or PT System. The TT or PT System creates two methods to compensate teachers and two levels of employment, one based on tenure, one based on performance. In some states this proposal may require legislative action to alter the current tenure laws to accommodate an alternative compensation system.

Teachers opting for the Tenure Track (TT) aspect of the proposed TT or PT System would continue to enjoy certain benefits:

- Security of employment
- Compensation guarantees of the single salary schedule
- Retention of tenure status
- Working conditions according to the then existing union agreement
- Business as usual for them

Teachers who choose the Performance Track would have other benefits:

- Modified or extended school year
- Variable assignments
- Per diem compensation well above the single salary schedule
- Individual contract of employment with the board
- No tenure provisions
- Retention of all other state and national statutes dealing with fair employment practices
- Compensation not a function of years of experience or degrees
- Two opportunities during employment years to opt out of the PT program at the end of a given period and be placed back on the Tenure Track without any loss of benefits, including seniority (those opting out would also have a second opportunity to reenter the PT program)
- Continued employment in the Performance Track contingent upon performance
- Evaluation not subject to negotiations since this is a personal service contract with the board of education

Those in the PT System would be paid a higher per diem than those in the TT System. The higher wages would be compensated for by moderating the increases in compensation in the TT System. The goal of the system is to make it cost neutral while compensating teachers on a more equitable basis.

Positive Aspects of a Pay-for-Performance System of Compensation

- First, it does not require an assessment of teacher performance before he or she enters the program.
- Second, every teacher has the opportunity to enter the program and demonstrate his or her talent.
- Third, all teachers have two opportunities to enter and leave the PT program if it is not to their liking. Those in the program will receive their first assessment at the semester break or midyear as to whether or not they are qualified to remain in the program the following year. Once accepted into the program, the compensation is determined based on the level of performance and work assignment.

Merit Pay Is Not a Viable Option

There is no risk involved for the teacher in that he or she has two chances to enter or opt out of the program and still retain the right to return to the Tenure Track aspect of the program with no loss of seniority or contracted benefits under the union and board agreement.

My experience has been that, in general, superintendents are not strong advocates for merit pay as a way to compensate outstanding teachers. While they may support the concept of differentiated pay, in reality they find merit pay to be too controversial and cumbersome to manage. Merit pay pits one professional against another. Because the administration makes the sole decision as to whether or not a teacher receives merit compensation, it sets both the administration and teaching staff at odds with one another.

The self-selection of the PT System eliminates much of the anger associated with merit pay. It preserves tenure as an option and it provides teachers with more control over their livelihood. For the taxpayer, it has the advantage of maintaining the same salary budget, but rewards teachers based on performance, an approach to compensation that many citizens understand and would appreciate. The Performance Track respects the union, protects tenure, and makes no effort to undermine its work.

Whatever efforts are made to negotiate an optional compensation system, it is vital that both parties be in substantial agreement. Unions and boards are players in the most important enterprise in the nation, an enterprise from which every other professional occupation emerges. Without successful schools, there is little hope for the nation.

My experience is that working with a strong, professional local union is far better than working with a weak one. With the former you could build a trusting relationship, an arrangement upon which any new compensation effort must be founded.

A final thought is offered relative to academic freedom for all teachers. One of the positive aspects of tenure is that over many decades it has provided academic freedom for teachers. While teachers have certain responsibilities to students and need to take care not to unduly influence them with their personal values and politics, they also have the right to express themselves in other professional venues without the threat of retaliation. Teachers who opt to work under the Performance Track System will be employed under a personal services contract with a board. Regardless of other conditions of employment, the PT teachers must enjoy the same academic freedom as those working under the TT System.

Key Chapter 12 Ideas

I propose a "Tenure Track or Performance Track" System.

The Performance Track compensation is better than Tenure Track compensation.

Performance Track allows for movement in and out of the system twice.

Compensation should be based on ability and contribution.

The single-salary schedule institutionalizes inertia.

Performance Track preserves the security of tenure for those who choose it.

The Performance Track System would foster improved relations with taxpayers.

Outstanding teachers should be compensated at a higher rate of pay.

13

Strategy Number 7: Performance-Based Compensation for Superintendents

---

Model Superintendent Contract Left Wanting

IN 1968 I NEGOTIATED MY FIRST contract as superintendent of schools with a board of education. That contract was one page long. It referenced only salary, health insurance, starting date, length of the contract, and a residency requirement. There was no language regarding renewal, termination, assessment, benefits, annuity, life insurance, and other benefits that are so common in contracts today. Importantly, it did not contain performance-based compensation language.

Within two years, with the assistance of seven colleagues and an attorney, a "model contract" had been developed applicable to other state superintendents. Initially, the state association of school superintendents was not interested in endorsing the model contract, but within a year it agreed to support efforts to distribute it to its members. The model contract allowed all superintendents to negotiate effectively with boards of education regarding compensation, length of contract, and many other conditions of employment. The contract was groundbreaking in terms of identifying those "other conditions of employment."

The next step was to approach the state association of boards of education to elicit its blessing. This was not an easy task since many aspects of the model contract that gave protection to superintendents would not necessarily be seen in a positive light by the state association of boards of education. At the time, the association had an executive director who understood how a clearly written contract could serve to avoid misunderstanding between boards and superintendents and would quietly assist both parties to peacefully sever relationships when necessary. With the director's support the association adopted the model contract.

What does this model contract have to do with performance-based compensation? As stated, it did not include performance-based compensation. This was a major failing, although at the time it was not seen as such. As a search consultant for fifteen years, I came across many contracts that were modeled after that which was adopted by the state superintendents association and the state boards of education association and none contained performance-based compensation language. In the hundred or more searches I conducted there was not a single case of a board tying compensation directly to performance. Several boards inquired as to the idea's feasibility, two or three explored the idea, and others made unsuccessful attempts, but none created a direct link between compensation and performance.

That is not to say that other consultants may have not have worked with districts in which there was a performance-based compensation plan for the superintendent. Most likely there are a few in existence in Connecticut. The point, however, is that they are not common. Basically, from 1968 through 2008, some forty years, there was no major effort by individual superintendents in my state to endorse performance-based compensation.

Tying compensation to performance was not an idea of the moment in 1969, but it certainly is today, given the state of public education. However, it is an issue that most superintendents apparently wish to keep at arm's length, both for themselves and their employees.

Essential Elements of a Superintendent Contract

Almost every contract put into use after 1969 in my home state did, however, include two essential conditions that were of prime importance to superintendents. There were many other important aspects in the contract, but these two were the most critical. The first was the process by which a contract of employment was extended or renewed. Initially, this was not a condition that boards were interested in but, as the competition for quality superintendents increased, boards began to make this concession. Seemingly every superintendent wanted some version of a contract that automatically extended itself so that there was always a guaranteed period of employment from three to five years depending upon the state.

The second essential condition in the contract was compensation and the conditions pertaining to how and when it was established. Superintendents were interested in establishing compensation for the full term of the contract and in that way guaranteeing themselves a salary regardless of their track record during the period of the contract. Given a three-to-five-year employment contract and a fixed, guaranteed salary that was unrelated to success was an ideal position for a superintendent to be in. It was an outstanding position for marginal performers to be in. Some contracts called for establishing an exact salary figure for each year while others used a percentage increase. Still others tied superintendent compensation to salary settlements of teachers, administrators, or both. Whatever the system of settling on a compensation figure, it worked to the advantage of superintendents. Whenever a board agreed to this system of payment, it effectively eliminated performance as a method of determining compensation.

It is difficult to judge what percentage of boards settled salary beyond the first year, but we can assume that many did not. Some of the boards I worked with were inclined to negotiate salary each year regardless of the length of the contract. In so doing, they believed, erroneously, that they were engaged in a performance-based compensation situation. As noted earlier, no other contractual condition was important if those dealing with contract renewal and compensation were not included. However, in my experience, few contracts tied compensation to performance.

Coupling Pay Directly with Student Success

Many superintendents will suggest that their compensation, if not directly tied to performance, is indirectly tied to performance in that if a board is satisfied with what he or she has accomplished during the year, it can reflect its pleasure by increasing salary and benefits. Others will state, for example, that if test scores in the district have risen even slightly that the board can increase their salary above the going percentage rate being granted throughout the state. Both of these positions are valid, but miss the point.

Performance-based compensation clearly implies that there is a direct connection between the improvement of all students' performance and what the superintendent is paid for achieving that improvement. It also implies that there is a direct relationship between what students do not learn and what a superintendent is not paid! The fact is that under most current compensation arrangements, a superintendent's salary is rarely decreased if test scores remain the same or decline. This is especially true if the superintendent holds a multi-year contract where the compensation is established for the full length of the contract. In fact, most contracts I have seen include specific language that denies the board the right to reduce the level of compensation during the term of the contract. This is a common clause in almost all contracts of employment between a superintendent and a board of education.

Why is this? What is it about the educational environment that guarantees employees compensation even if there is no significant gain in student achievement? Why are school superintendents immune from the consequences of operating an underachieving school?

It is fair to ask why lagging student achievement in a school system has no serious impact on what superintendents are paid. While outstanding student scores may result in a more significant pay raise for a superintendent, I can think of no case where a superintendent's salary was reduced in keeping with average or declining scores.

Until compensation for school superintendents is linked to what students learn, education will struggle to improve. The reason is simple: under what is best described as a guaranteed compensation plan, there is no incentive to be daring, to be "out of the box," to be different, to experiment. Quite the contrary; a guaranteed salary will create an environment in which a superintendent is encouraged to be conformist, middle of the road, quiet, and invisible. This may be the road to somewhere but is certainly not the road to improvement.

Resistance to Performance Pay

One of the arguments against performance pay is that because the improvement in student achievement is the result of efforts by hundreds, if not thousands, of teachers, administrators, and other support staff, how can a board of education in good conscience reward only the superintendent? The answer is that in most every other profession, the leader who is able to deploy human and financial resources in such a manner to make the organization successful is the person who is rewarded. It is the superintendent's drive, passion, talent, work ethic, and creativity that makes it possible for all employees to work at an optimum level, and to share in the rewards which result when the entire enterprise is successful.

There are other arguments against performance-based compensation. For example:

- How can a superintendent be held accountable for students who arrive at school with no basic language skills?
- How can a superintendent be held accountable without authority to hire and fire?
- How is a superintendent expected to deal with the poverty issue?
- How does she design schools to compensate for what is lacking at home?

These and other questions bring us full circle regarding the leadership issue. I can speak from my own experience, and that of dozens of superintendents with whom I worked closely during my active years as a superintendent. Not often spoken but certainly known to superintendents is the fact that just about any intelligent administrator from any level of the organization can be successful at being a superintendent, and many of them are. Many high school principals in my state became superintendents without any other central office experience. One does not need an additional sixty hours of university courses to qualify as an effective superintendent.

Running a small or medium-sized district is not much different than managing a large school. True, there is a size issue, but this is not a real handicap. With decent management skills and a good central office staff, most administrators are able to successfully run a district. The question, however, is whether this person is capable of leading a district. It is the "leading" part that is the issue. Many can run, but few can lead!

Compensation Will Decline for Some Under a Pay-for-Performance System

Hundreds if not thousands of school districts across the nation are managed by superintendents who would rarely earn a pay raise if they were employed under performance-based contracts that directly tied the success of all students to compensation. It is comfortable to slide along in your position when you have a guaranteed salary increase and an extended contract. And if and when you sense that your employment status is somewhat questionable and that your annual renewal is being questioned, you simply move along to another district and promise still another board that you will improve instruction.

It is important that we constantly remind ourselves that fifty years after *Sputnik* and after expending vast amounts of money, we still have schools that underachieve.

Every board of education in the nation needs to place its superintendent on a performance-based compensation plan. School budget increases would be much easier to achieve if administrators and teachers were paid for performance and not for simply making it through another year. This would be a situation that the taxpayer could relate to. Such plans may not have been needed in past decades, but they are essential now.

Clear, unambiguous student success performance targets need to be established so every board and their superintendents can reach these goals. There is no other option. Students cannot wait any longer for success to reach them.

After reading this chapter, some will ask, "Why, if principals are also a key partner in raising student achievement levels, are they not compensated in the same way as proposed for superintendents?" It is a fair question. The answer is that there also should be a differentiated salary system for principals. The more successful among them should be compensated for their achievement. The question is how to make distinctions and when. Rather than use a performance-based system that is the same as that of the superintendent, I am of the opinion that any system for principals should be a hybrid that employs elements from both the teacher and superintendent models and is tailored to local conditions. Until a system is in place for the superintendent, it would not be appropriate to begin to design a system for principals. It is for the superintendent to take the lead by being first in line with a performance-based compensation system.

Key Chapter 13 Ideas

Boards must adopt true performance-based compensation for superintendents.

It is a system of payment that is appropriate for the times.

Compensation should be directly tied to documented improvement in student achievement.

Annual increases in pay without improvement in student learning are unjustified.

Superintendents should be the first employee group to accept merit pay.

14

Three Essential Questions for Boards of Education and School Superintendents

Important Questions Demand Honest Answers

THIS BOOK SHOULD ENCOURAGE THE reader to frame questions that are related to the seven strategies. For example, the chapter on recruiting cannot help but raise the question with the reader as to the ethics or lack thereof at play in his or her own school district's recruiting system. The chapter on fiscal responsibility should raise a question about the way priorities are established and how funds are allocated to different school programs and activities.

The chapter on educational leadership should lead one to wonder if those who run the district or lead a school building are academic leaders or simply middle-level managers. The two chapters on performance-based compensation, one for teachers and one for administrators, should raise multiple questions as to how school districts pay their employees.

The chapter on staff levels will hopefully make the reader question what impact large class sizes have on student learning. The chapter on boards of education should make one consider who is being elected to run schools and protect children. And so it goes with every chapter; each should raise provocative questions. Certainly, the overarching question is why schools are not successfully educating all students.

For me, this analysis raises three questions that should be of interest to parents and citizens. These are questions that need to be answered by those in control. Some readers will disagree with my selection of questions. They may have others that are more important. The fact is that all readers should compose their own questions and ask those in power to answer them directly.

My three questions address three troubling issues for me: first, why we do not invest heavily in teaching every single one of our children to read; second, why we build large factories and then call them schools; and third, why we pay the most marginally competent teacher the same salary at the best teacher. These questions are developed more fully below.

Question Number One

Why, in the elementary grades in particular, have we allowed class sizes to rise to levels that are well above what educators know are desirable for all students to achieve success? There is ample evidence to demonstrate that in order to effectively teach reading to all students, in particular those who come to school with limited language proficiency, class sizes need to be held to under twenty. Many advocates are lobbying for still lower ratios. In spite of this evidence, school systems continue to bundle children into neat packages of twenty-five or thirty, often more, and then expect teachers to bring all students up to proficiency.

This failure on the part of boards of education and school superintendents to reduce class sizes in the primary grades is typical of educators spending much of their time and resources attempting to solve problems of their own making. Students who fall behind in the early grades will undoubtedly experience failure throughout their school years. Students who are unable to read will be unable to succeed in any academic subject. The most common answer is that funds are not available to add that extra teacher in any given grade to reduce class sizes while, on the other hand, they will continue to be available for questionable electives at the high school level or interscholastic sports at the middle school level. School districts almost always can find tuition money for high school students to attend a specialized magnet school out of district while ignoring the need for an additional reading teacher in grade one.

Each time a school district turns its back on reliable solutions to the teaching of reading to all students in the early grades, it simply postpones the day when these students will fall behind other students in their grade and then require expensive remedial assistance. Some of these students will never complete high school and they will become part of the uneducated adult population in the United States.

Teaching services are not unlike infrastructure needs; you pay now or you pay later, but you will undoubtedly pay. Any attempt to bring students up to grade as they fall further behind and grow older is not a guaranteed road to success. These students are at high risk for dropping out of school and entering our society with limited skills. Then the finger-pointing begins, but the finger is never aimed in the correct direction. It defies logic that boards of education and school superintendents have not rallied around the need to reduce class sizes in the early grades. It is one of the most obvious ways to guarantee educational success.

Is a major effort to reduce class sizes in all elementary schools not a "big idea" worthy of the attention of a board and superintendent? The cost of ignorance is profound both for students who fail and for society in general.

Question Number Two

Why have superintendents and other leaders in education not fought fiercely for small high schools? There has been much research generated surrounding the benefits of small schools, especially high schools. Early efforts were made by the Coalition of Essential Schools with its emphasis on "personalization" within a school. Several other national organizations have addressed this issue.

Recognizing that not all districts can afford to rebuild schools, efforts were made at internal reorganization that afforded big schools the option of resembling small schools; that is, dispersing a large student body into small units, usually through the use of "houses" within a school, each with its own administration and staff. It was and remains a worthwhile alternative to existing large schools.

On the other hand, when school districts across the nation have a need to build a new comprehensive high school to accommodate an increasing population, they invariably continue to build large institutional facilities in spite of the evidence that small schools create a more effective learning environment for students. The reason for building large schools is financial. Yet it does not go without notice that most new magnet schools are small, with limited enrollments. It is interesting that, on one hand, boards and superintendents are willing to accept the concept of "small" for magnet schools while, on the other, they will not advocate for small high schools in their own community.

Is it not a worthy "big idea" for a board of education and school superintendent to advocate for the same environment for its comprehensive high school that is afforded those students who attend magnet schools?

Question Number Three

Why have boards of education not mounted a strong offense to alter the way in which they compensate teachers? Seventy percent of a district's budget is committed to teacher salaries, and within the universe of teachers the most outstanding teacher on the staff is paid no more than the least capable teacher! Historically, merit pay has not been an effective tool to unhinge the single-salary schedule. In spite of the best efforts to make it a viable alternative to the single-salary schedule, it is too controversial to be effective. Yet at the university level there is some evidence that union-supported merit pay does exist.

The taxpayer cries out for some relief from the impact of the single-salary schedule and its inexorable annual increase without any significant improvement in student achievement. Is it fair that another year of marginal service should yield an increase in salary? Is it right that another degree earned, one that is unrelated to a teacher's assignment, should be rewarded by an increase in compensation? For example, is there any research that can validate that a master's degree in administration earned by a guidance counselor improves his or her ability to counsel students? Is it appropriate that course work that is not approved administratively be eligible for payment when it has no relationship to the assignment? This should be closely monitored and always require prior approval.

It is no secret in education that many degrees are earned simply to increase the compensation to teachers and administrators and not to improve instruction. With the advent of Internet courses, school districts find themselves remunerating teachers who receive credit and degrees from questionable colleges and universities. Credits are earned at an alarming rate. All Internet courses need to be examined to determine if the requirements for credit match those of courses provided on-site.

It is time for boards of education and school superintendents to engage in a serious effort to identify alternative compensation plans that reward an individual according to his or her documented contribution and on the quality of work. Is this not the stuff that "big ideas" are made of?

Key Chapter 14 Ideas

I note three essential questions regarding the book's topics.

Readers are encouraged to raise their own essential questions.

Essential questions should then be addressed to the local board of education.

Answers to these questions provide insight into a board's dedication and commitment.

15

A Word about Chapters 16 and 17

I HAVE IDENTIFIED SEVEN STRATEGIES THAT, if fully implemented by a board of education and its school superintendent, have the potential to make all schools successful. They are:

1. A powerful board of education
2. Academic leadership provided by the superintendent of schools
3. Instructional power at the building level
4. A powerful and equitable recruiting system
5. Appropriate staffing levels
6. Tenure Track or Performance Track options for teachers
7. Performance-based compensation for superintendents

Six of the seven are controlled by a board of education. The seventh, Tenure Track or Performance Track, is only partially controlled by the board in that it must negotiate this with the teacher unions. All seven determine how a board will function, what the superintendent is expected to do, what role the principal will play, what form recruiting will take, and so on.

However, there are three other important players in a school district's quest to be successful:

- Colleges of education
- State certification agencies
- Parents

They are not considered strategies in that the board of education has no control over them. A board can attempt to influence each of them, but in the final analysis they will do as they please. Each employs its unique guidance system to determine direction. Nevertheless, I would be remiss not to discuss the roles that each of the three parties play in the educational enterprise.

Two of them, colleges of education and state certification agencies, are the subject of chapter 16. The third one, parents, is the subject of chapter 17.

16

Colleges of Education and State Certification Agencies Are Connected to Unsuccessful Schools

---

Two Organizations Capable of Dramatically Reforming Education

THROUGHOUT THIS BOOK, I HAVE identified the reasons elementary and secondary education have not lived up to their promise. There remain far too many students who are starved for a quality education. One way for a school system to address this shortcoming is to invest in the seven strategies. If fully implemented, they present an opportunity for a school district to become successful or to improve its level of success. In order to guarantee success over the long run, however, two other highly bureaucratic enterprises need to participate in reform. Because they are closely intertwined, the discussion about them is interwoven.

As an author and educator, I continue to be disappointed at the credit requirements that aspiring teachers and administrators must earn for a graduate degree in education. The reaction is also due in part to the course requirements needed for purposes of gaining certification as a teacher or administrator. I believe it fair to conclude that if teachers, administrators, and school superintendents are partially responsible for the lack of student success, then it follows that the colleges and universities that trained them and the state agencies that credentialed them are also partly responsible.

Teacher training institutions are able to justify the credits needed for an undergraduate degree in education, since the credits count is not unlike those for other degrees. However, they would have a difficult time justifying the many credits needed for graduate degrees, in particular those required for an administrative degree.

Cash Flow Takes Priority

Graduate schools of education are a major source of cash flow for colleges and universities. School of education professors are probably not on the high end of the college or university pay scale, and the facilities needed to teach are minimal. Many courses are taught off-site in school districts. In many cases they are taught in districts where the superintendent is an adjunct professor at the college or university offering the courses. Most of the time there is no expense to the college for the use of facilities. Unlike courses in other disciplines, education courses at the graduate level have no need for laboratories, laboratory assistants, or expensive equipment. The use of adjuncts is widespread and their use is economical since they are paid on a per course basis and often receive no benefits.

As a result of having earned two graduate degrees requiring ninety hours of course work, I am of the opinion that whatever knowledge one needs to acquire through graduate school work in educational administration can be learned through fewer courses; courses that are properly designed, highly condensed, and effectively assessed. Colleges and universities that train public school administrators border on being larcenous for requiring so many expensive courses. The more I reflect on my course work for the doctorate, I have difficulty identifying a single course I could not have done without. I could have easily become a superintendent based on my prior course work and experiences as a principal and assistant superintendent.

Training institutions appear to march in lockstep with state departments of education across the country that also contribute to credit inflation when they artificially create a scarcity of school administrators through questionable certification requirements. The increase in certification requirements creates a scarcity of administrators. This scarcity is compounded when certification agencies take other actions that make it difficult and cumbersome for administrators to move freely from state to state without having to become involved in a testing requirement. It shakes the confidence of everyone when a successful school superintendent in one state needs to take what amounts to an "entrance exam" and/or additional course work to gain employment in another state.

Many Certification Requirements Are Illogical

If one thinks about it, what is the logic in deciding that an outstanding and successful superintendent from California cannot work in Connecticut without taking the equivalent of a mini SAT exam? Who dreamed up the regulations in many states that prohibit a chief executive officer of a major corporation like Coca-Cola from running a public school system? If Leonard Bernstein was alive, many school systems in the country could not hire him permanently as a music teacher unless he either passed a test or engaged in course work! A skilled lab scientist from a major pharmaceutical company could not be hired as a science teacher in many states without meeting the same requirements noted above.

Clearly, this is a certification system that has lost its way. As one colleague noted, if certification officials are as smart as they think they are in establishing standards, why have "certified educators" across the country not stemmed the tide of school failures? The good news, if there is any, is that schools of education now have the opportunity to increase their cash flow by enrolling additional educators in another course to meet what many believe are bogus standards. State accreditation requirements create a "make work" environment for colleges and universities.

This book asserts that the most important of the seven strategies that are offered as methods to raise the success rate of schools is a board of education. It is also a fact that nothing will become reality without strong superintendent leadership. Unfortunately, modern university teachings are such that the "strong leader" concept has been swept aside for the more comfortable "collaborative" style of leadership. When committee decisions are made and consensus is required before implementation, it is small wonder that education has a built-in inertia that suppresses creative leadership.

This book is not intended to undermine the work of either schools of education or state certification agencies. There would be little value in such an effort and nothing to be gained from such an approach. However, colleges and universities that prepare our teachers and administrators need a wake-up call to the fact that their graduates are part of the reason we have a floundering public school system.

Schools of Education Educate a Number of Marginal Performers

During fifteen years as a search consultant, I examined thousands of applications from both experienced and aspiring superintendents. During that period I read writing samples, reviewed applications, and examined transcripts from many outstanding individuals who went on to successful careers. It would have made any student, teacher, or parent proud to know these individuals. Fortunate are the districts that employed them.

The bad news is that among those thousands of individuals there was an unacceptably large number who were incapable of composing an articulate writing sample, whose applications were incomplete and could not be processed, and whose transcripts displayed an astonishing lack of outstanding academic success at the undergraduate level. These individuals had no place in education, certainly not in leadership roles. Yet they entered and graduated from schools of education and many went on, one way or another, to managing if not leading school systems. All of these candidates, the outstanding and the marginally competent, were the products of schools of education.

Blame for this situation cannot be attributed solely to schools of education. It is true that they graduate those who should never have been in a program to begin with, they require too many courses, and they have courses that are not relevant. However, it raises the question as to whether schools of education convince certification bureaus to add more course requirements and thus increase college credits required for certification or if they are the beneficiaries of expansionist thinking at such bureaus. In any event, both institutions shoulder responsibility for some of the blame for underperforming schools.

If Only They Would Lead

The irony in all of this is that both institutions are capable of leading educational reform. The fact is that they should be the vanguard of dramatic reform. They hold powerful positions in education, have influential friends in government, possess intellectual horsepower in their ranks, have the funding to hire creative geniuses, have the ear of state education commissioners, control substantial resources, are connected to the media, and are listened to by state legislative bodies. They possess all of the qualities and resources to be the major players in educational reform! Instead, both organizations spend their energy and intellect on details and more details.

By their bureaucratic actions, they have condemned themselves to becoming educational mechanics rather than leaders and designers. Instead of accepting marginal graduate students and building barriers to certification, they should be promoting new ideas, creating new visions, bringing certification into the twenty-first century, and taking a leadership role to help public schools. Instead of attracting more qualified candidates for educational leadership, their current protocols discourage many from entering the profession.

If colleges and certification agencies wish to assist in attracting talented individuals to education, they need to reduce barriers to easy movement between states and ease the restrictions that prohibit successful business leaders from operating schools. Who better than they to take the leadership in promoting performance-based compensation and a return to the "strong leader" concept?

When compensation for performance increases dramatically as a result of quality superintendents meeting student achievement targets, more outstanding men and women will enter the profession. The states that take a leadership role in reform will be those that attract the most talented educators. Education needs the equivalent of free trade. It must open the marketplace for more outstanding individuals to lead our schools.

Key Chapter 16 Ideas

Schools of education require too many irrelevant courses for a graduate degree.

They inadequately train teachers and administrators for public school positions.

Since they train them, they are partially responsible for lack of student success.

State certification bureaus have created a monster of certification systems.

Archaic regulations prevent the outstanding from entering the profession.

Both institutions should be reformers not conformists.

Both, possessing such enormous talent, need to take the initiative to institute major reform.

17

Parents As a Power Source

PARENTS MAY NOT BE ONE OF THE seven strategies that a board of education has control over, but they comprise a formidable force in education. If a board of education and superintendent in any community, anywhere, does not comprehend this, they are in for the surprise of their professional lives. The change in the typical parent role during the past twenty-five years has been nothing short of revolutionary. Parents understand with great clarity that the schools belong to them and that teachers and administrators work for them.

Parents have significant influence over what occurs in the schoolhouse. This influence has had a profound impact on the way schools are operated. Many a principal and teacher have been driven out of a district by vocal parents who disagree with a school's philosophy or teaching strategies. In some ways, parents are a more potent force in driving marginal teachers and administrators out of a district than is the superintendent. Influential and active parents spend more time in any one school than a typical superintendent and therefore have better insights into what is occurring than do central office personnel.

Not having control over parents means that the board of education and the superintendent must engage parents in a way that differs from their interaction with the staff. The starting point for them should be to identify ways in which parents are a positive force and ways that they are impediments to making a school successful. Parents can be a positive force for the following reasons:

- They love to volunteer to work in classrooms and media centers.
- They are generally supportive of a caring principal and teaching staff.

- They want to humanize schools and instruction.
- They are strong supporters of school budgets.
- They want a principal who exhibits intellectual curiosity.
- They want teachers who are fair.
- They are successful fund raisers.
- They see success as more than test scores.

The principal who has the ability to harness the energy and interests of parents will have created a secondary workforce. He or she will also have developed a powerful support system for the school.

Parents can be a negative force for these reasons:

- They are aggressive and forceful and not easily put off.
- They can be intimidating to teachers and administrators.
- They often have a "my kid only" attitude.
- They can antagonize taxpayers over budget increases.
- They can mobilize opposition to administrative action quickly.
- They can spread rumors.
- They can interfere with the workings of the school day.

The principal who is able to minimize the negative aspects of parent behavior and emphasize the positive aspects will have an easier time promoting success in the school.

Parents Are No Longer Intimidated by Educators

It was mentioned earlier that there was a time when parents were frightened of teachers and administrators and left the schooling of their children to them. It was a case of "the teacher knows best." Because of that situation, parents began to exert their influence in schools across the country and in every demographic setting. Parents now know that teachers do not always know what is best for children.

While there is some basis to believe that urban and rural parents do not participate in school life to the extent that suburban parents do, it does not mean that they are not interested or not influential. Often, they will use advocacy groups to express their concerns. Thus they, too, are a formidable force. It was because parents were uncertain that teachers were sufficiently talented to deal with their children that parents decided to get involved. It was not altruism that brought parents into schools; it was the fear that their children would be overlooked!

But the question remains: what occurred that made parents no longer fearful of teachers and made them willing to confront school administrators and board of education members when they were not satisfied with the quality of schooling? How did they become such a positive force for change on one hand or a powerful foe on the other hand? I identify three primary events.

First, there was and remains a strong feminist movement nationwide that has motivated women to take strong leadership roles in all walks of life, but particularly in schools. Many women are former teachers. Schools provide an opportunity for women to become involved since they have easy access to schools. It is the one institution where they have been welcomed. And, in those instances when parents, both male and female, may not be welcomed, the law provides them with legal access.

Second, many parents have been employed in business and know how organizations work and how to work the organization. Many of them held impressive positions and supervised employees. Others ran their own companies. Many remain active in business while their children are in school. They are not fearful of asking questions, making inquiries, examining data, and using their influence and that of others to make things work for them and their children.

Third, there are more women students in school at all levels up to and including graduate schools. They constitute an enormous, well-educated universe. In many cases they come to their local schools in their role as parents with a far more impressive educational background than those who teach their children and who manage their schools. Parents are no longer an undereducated class seeking an audience with educators. Those days are long gone and gone forever.

Parent Volunteers and an Expectation of Favoritism

Not all parents have the opportunity to do volunteer work in schools because they either have to work in an income-producing job to help support their family or they have so much to do as stay-at-home moms. The fact that they are not able to be in schools on a regular basis is no reason their children should be denied the same care as all other children. Conversely, parents who spend a great deal of time in school should not use their position to gain an advantage for their children over those whose parents are unable to be in school on a regular basis.

Teacher and administrative favoritism displayed toward some children because their parents are active in school is a situation that principals must guard against. Every child has the right to the same services and considerations. There must be no exceptions. The case was made earlier that an "insider" should be given no preference in applying for a position in the district. The same philosophy must be in place in dealing with the children of parents who are on "the inside."

In several chapters, I referenced principals in a positive light. I have a bias towards them and believe they are the most important administrators in a school system. The fact is that without capable building-level administrators there can be no successful school system. That cannot be said for any other position. Boards of education and school superintendents should rely heavily on principals to determine how best to work with parents. They must lend their considerable authority in support of those actions taken by a principal. Second-guessing the decisions of those who keep a system on track is not leadership.

Key Chapter 17 Ideas

Parents believe that schools belong to them.
They know better than the administration who the marginal teachers are.
Parents are able to have teachers and administrators removed.
They can be a powerful positive force.
They can be a powerful negative force.
Parents are no longer fearful of teachers or administrators.
Many are better educated than some staff.

Epilogue

"You're late. I expected you earlier."

"The meeting started late. Many members wanted to meet the speaker before he spoke."

"Usually they wait until the speech is over."

"True, but his topics had generated sufficient interest that some members wanted to meet to him early. The session started late and ended late because of the questions both during his speech and after."

"And?"

"And it was an excellent session. I have to say that it was not a speech per se. It was more conversational in tone. There was a lot of interaction between the speaker and the audience. The members were very professional. The speaker was reserved and respectful of his audience. He answered every question and was not evasive. If anyone expected a rabble-rousing revolutionary, they were disappointed. He had points to make and made them. I couldn't help but be impressed with how carefully he listened to every question. Bottom line is that he was good."

"Right, but, how about the strategies? What were the ideas?"

"I brought you the handout that lists the seven of them with considerable background. He made a lot of sense whether or not you agreed with all seven strategies. However, two or three were really controversial with the group."

"I am looking at the list. Which were the controversial ones?"

"I think the most controversial was the one dealing with inequitable, unethical, and unprofessional hiring practices. He was adamant that school systems will never dramatically improve or reform themselves if the hiring process is flawed. As he said, if you employ the wrong workers, it is all downhill from there. You spend time and money fixing a problem you created. He made the claim, controversial with some members, that you can never improve a marginal employee."

"Do you agree with that?"

"I do happen to agree with him. It has been my experience that attempting to improve an employee's performance is a case of throwing good money after bad. A business enterprise would never fall into this trap. He really touched a soft spot with some of the members when he mentioned favoritism in hiring. It caused some stirring in the audience. We know that it occurs in some districts, even those close to home."

"Is it really that bad in some districts?"

"You have to think so. However, he made a really important point as to why it is so important to hire carefully and ethically, a point that most of us do not think about. The fact is that the minority students of today will be the majority adult population in twenty to thirty years, perhaps sooner. And it is a fact that as a percentage of students currently enrolled in our public schools, they are the most undereducated of our population through no fault of their own. If schools fail them, they fail the country. The minorities are the leaders of tomorrow. It is for that reason that those who teach or lead these students must be chosen by ability not by favoritism or political connections."

"What were the other controversial strategies?"

"There were two others that caused some upset. The first had to do with boards of education. Again, he made a strong case that most boards do not use their authority to bring about major improvement in schools and have relegated that responsibility to superintendents who possess no real authority. You have to read the material because he presents a lot of detail. The interesting thing is I am not certain whether boards will be pleased or displeased at the idea that they should have a greater presence in school systems. I do know that the superintendents in the audience had mixed feeling about this strategy."

"It is my opinion that board of education members will never be innovators for the very reason that their primary goal is to be reelected. My experience is that they have sold out to parents and could care less about the taxpayer. You put a half dozen parents in the audience demanding a change and the board thinks of them as a mob and yields to them. Board members have no strength of character."

"They are supposed to represent parents, not taxpayers."

"They must represent the entire community. They are spending our money!"

"That is a point he also drives home in the book. But the fact is boards must do what is right for students."

"And the other controversial strategy?"

"In retrospect, this one may be tied with the hiring practice strategy for first place. He believes that most superintendents are great at managing schools but many do not fill the role of academic leader. He certainly is not the first educational writer to take this position, but his criticism may stick because he has the credentials to back it up. He has walked the talk in his previous life."

"When you reflect on the overall theme of his work, what is it?"

"It is what many of us have thought about but did not implement. Educators are so mired in old school traditions that we have suppressed innovation. Most of us lack the courage to be risk takers. Consequently, schools have failed to become outstanding learning institutions. Nationally, the public schools simply warehouse a good percentage of students. Added to the equation is the fact that collaborative leadership has effectively outlawed the strong leader concept, resulting in management by committee."

"Too bad parents and taxpayers could not have heard him. Whether he is right or wrong, it sounds as though he has raised some serious issues that everyone should be concerned about. I'd like to meet him."

"I have no doubt we will hear more from him. He is not going to go away, that's for sure. He noted that he is working on a sequel."

Genesis of the Book

THE IDEAS EXPRESSED IN THIS BOOK were originally developed as a basis for a proposed state-level audit system, the purpose being to examine why underperforming school districts are unable to bring about significant gains in student achievement. In spite of vast financial resources that have been provided to schools over the last five decades, beginning with the political and scientific panic following the launching of the Soviet Union's *Sputnik,* insufficient progress has been made in improving education for all students. The results of the proposed audit would answer the question as to why schools fail. That data would be used by the district to introduce reform efforts.

I was interested in devising an alternative way to assess a district's commitment to excellence, one based on the degree to which the above-listed seven strategies were in play, all seven of which are people-based. As a result of several decades of work in education, and fundamental to my system of improvement, is that any investigation of a school system should be viewed through lenses different from those currently being employed.

The protocols for the audit were straightforward:

- Collect and examine detailed, verifiable data appropriate to each of the seven strategies.
- Present objective findings without educational jargon.
- Be truthful with the data.

Throughout the book, I have expressed that the need to improve instruction for all students is of the highest priority in our society and this must remain the primary goal of the public school system. Therefore, I viewed it as imperative that an audit and analysis of school performance be undertaken in all schools in which students are not scoring at the proficiency level, with special emphasis on individual schools and students in subgroups who were underperforming.

Educators know what students need to learn; the problem is what to do if they do not learn. Nagging in the minds of all educators is the realization that proficiency is low-level achievement at best. Meanwhile, the richest nation on the planet is struggling to reach this minimum level of proficiency for all students in spite of what might be considered Herculean efforts. It can be reasonably concluded that many of those efforts and much of the billions of dollars expended have been misplaced.

As noted in the introduction, my philosophy is that educators need to examine underperforming schools and districts through the lens of personnel shortcomings rather than programmatic shortcomings. Each of the seven strategies is people-based. This focus is based on my extensive experience with over 100 school systems and in my multiple roles as superintendent, search consultant, general consultant, and many interim superintendent assignments. I am committed to the principle that improvement in student performance must be people-driven.

With deeply held ideas as to how school systems should be judged in order to improve, I utilized the basic outline of the audit proposal and developed this book. The ideas are intended to be inspiring and not overly controversial.

Notes on Terminology

THROUGHOUT THE BOOK I USE THE WORD *success* as it relates to students. Webster's Ninth New Collegiate Dictionary defines it as a "favorable or desired outcome." Within the context of this book is it is also meant to be a "favorable or desired outcome."

The larger question is, what does that mean as it relates to education? Simply stated, it means that every student, in every demographic niche, in every school across the nation, in every class or grade, in cities, suburbs, and rural settings, in rich and poor communities, will be offered the highest attainable quality of instruction such that they are able to achieve at legitimate, challenging standards established for any course or grade. It implies that the standards of instruction are not dumbed down, adjusted, or made socially correct in order that all can achieve at some artificially created acceptable level.

Excellence/Excellent

I also use the terms *excellence* and *excellent* throughout the book in reference to the type of school and/or quality of instruction that all students should expect to experience. Webster defines *excellence* as "a valuable quality" and *excellent* as "first class."

The underlying thought throughout this book is that all aspects of the educational enterprise need to be first class, especially the instruction offered to students and the culture of the school that determines how well students will learn. A major concern expressed is that many students never have the opportunity to experience first-class instruction.

In reference to students, *excellence* and *excellent* are used to denote the highest quality of instruction possible. When used in reference to a school, they are used to describe the most desirable school setting and supportive culture that is attainable.

Superintendents and District Size and Complexity

Throughout this book, reference is made to the position of "superintendent," the highest-ranking educator in the district and the person responsible for implementing board of education policies. The size and complexity of a district will determine what roles the superintendent will play. These roles will vary significantly from district to district.

In a small or medium-sized district, the superintendent is assumed to be the academic leader although in reality that is often not the case. In a large, urban district, the superintendent is essentially a politician and chief administrative officer or chief operating officer, and the instructional leadership role is delegated to assistants and deputies, who act much like a superintendent might act in small or medium-sized districts. In large consolidated, regional, and county systems, the superintendent will also delegate instructional leadership to others. That said, regardless of the size of a district, a superintendent can delegate duties and responsibilities to subordinates, but cannot and must not delegate accountability.

Boards of Education

The term *board of education* is used to describe the governing body of a school system. The term differs from state to state. They may be referred to as school committees, boards of education, governing boards, boards of directors, boards of trustees, or others. Each serves the same function, which is to set policy for school systems, develop the district vision, create "big ideas," and employ a superintendent to lead the system.

Regional Differences in Budget Development

School systems across the country are organized in many different ways. In some parts of the nation, every community has its own school system, meaning that the physical boundaries of the community are the physical boundaries of the school district. In other places, schools are organized on a county basis. There are school systems that are comprised of portions of several communities. Within each of these configurations there may be regional school systems, charter schools, and magnet schools; sometimes they are organized for elementary schools, other times for secondary schools, and still others serve the entire K-12 population. Knowing America's love for independent thought, it is most likely that there are several other forms of school organization.

I mention the various school organizations because of the different formats that will be used in budget development within each one. In some cases the taxpayers are close to the action and in others they are kept at arm's length. In small communities taxpayers usually vote on the school budget, and in urban centers and county systems school budgets may simply be thrust upon them. Regional districts, magnet schools, and charter schools have still other mechanisms for approval.

Bibliography

Connecticut faces a school tax revolt. (2008, August 23). *Hartford Courant.*

Denver teachers object to changes in pay-for-performance plan. (2008, August 6). *The Wall Street Journal.*

Economic realities must be faced. (2009, January 13). *Hartford Courant.*

Eyes on school reform. (2008, August 21). *Hartford Courant,* p. A10.

Farrish, K. (2008, October 22). Schools chief gets extension, 3.5% pay raise. *Hartford Courant,* p. A19.

Farrish, K. (2009, January 7). Divided board rejects some new courses. *Hartford Courant,* p. A4.

Keating, C. (2009, January 13). The budget squeeze is on. *Hartford Courant,* p. A3.

Levy, C. (2008, December 26). Obama picks a moderate on education. *The Wall Street Journal,* p. A11.

Math reforms lead nowhere. (2008, August 18). *Hartford Courant.*

Mozdzer, J. (2008, November 28). Cuts might curb city school redesign plans. *Hartford Courant,* p. A19.

Mozdzer, J. (2008, December 5). Charter schools may buoy urban districts. *Hartford Courant,* p. A8.

Pandiscio, H. F. (2004). *Job hunting in education.* Lanham, MD: Scarecrow Education in partnership with the American Association of School Administrators.

Pandiscio, H. F. (2005). *Recruiting strategies for public schools.* Lanham, MD: Rowman & Littlefield Education in partnership with the American Association of School Administrators.

Reform launched in Hartford schools. (2008, August 24). *Hartford Courant.*

School board reform is the missing ingredient in education. (2008, March 6). *Herald Tribune.*

Sizer, T. R. (1984). *Horace's compromise.* Boston: Houghton Mifflin.

Sizer, T. R. (1994). Coalition of Essential Schools. Brown University.
Toppo, G. (2008, November 18). Big goals for teachers union. *USA Today*, p. 7D.
Tough contract bargaining. (2008, December 13). *Hartford Courant.*
Trying to ensure quality reading instruction. (2008, October 17). *Hartford Courant.*
Wills, G. (2008, August 21). Why strict schools work. *Hartford Courant.*
Wills, G. (2008, September 11). Drowning in pensions. *Hartford Courant.*

Index

About the Author

Herbert F. Pandiscio earned an undergraduate degree in business and economics, a master's degree in secondary education, and a doctorate in educational administration. During the period between earning his bachelor and advanced degrees, he served in the United States Army in a counterintelligence unit. He was superintendent of schools in Avon, Connecticut, for twenty-five years. Upon retirement from Avon he formed Herbert William Consulting, Inc., later known as Avon Educational Search Consultants, LLC, an administrative search firm specializing in identifying and hiring school superintendents, central office employees, and school administrators. For fifteen years he worked as a search consultant, private job coaching specialist, and interim superintendent of schools in numerous districts.

He brings experience to the many suggestions and ideas offered in this book through time spent as teacher, high school department chairman, assistant track coach, assistant principal, middle and high school principal, assistant superintendent for secondary education, superintendent of schools, interim superintendent of multiple school districts, general consultant, search consultant, and author of two previous books in education. His first book, *Job Hunting in Education*, chronicled the successes and failures of job seekers. Candidates will find it helpful in securing a position in education.

His second book, *Recruiting Strategies for Public Schools,* was developed for superintendents and human relations personnel to assist them in managing the many stages of the recruiting process. This book, *A Power Shift in Public*

Education, is written for all who wish to help stem the failures in our schools, but especially for:

Superintendents
Boards of Education
School administrators
Human relations directors
Schools of Education faculty
State certification personnel
Union leadership
Teachers
Parents
PTO/PTA officials
Local and state public officials
Taxpayers
Journalists
Organizations committed to educational reform

And for Joe and Janice Citizen, who are having trouble making ends meet and who have shouldered the financial burden of underwriting unfulfilled promises.